TRAVELING
THE GLOBE AND MAKING MEMORIES!

Travel Journal and Scrapbook

Write Planners and Notebooks

Copyright 2016

All Rights reserved. No part of this book may be reproduced or used in any way or form or by any means whether electronic or mechanical, this means that you cannot record or photocopy any material ideas or tips that are provided in this book.

My Travel Journal

Packing List

- ☐ Visa
- ☐ Passport
- ☐ Tickets
- ☐ ID's
- ☐ Credit Card
- ☐ Camera
- ☐ Chargers
- ☐ Sunglasses
- ☐ Shoes
- ☐ Slippers

Important Reminders

MY TRAVEL JOURNAL

Hotel Reservation :

Place to travel :

Contact Person/Contact number :

Travel Date :

Tour Guide :

Friends to see / visit :
-
-
-
-
-

Contact Person/Contact number :

Places to visti :
-
-
-
-
-
-

photo here

MY TRAVEL JOURNAL

Shopping list

Food Must Try

Food trip photo here

MY TRAVEL JOURNAL

the best part of this travel

unforgettable memories

journal

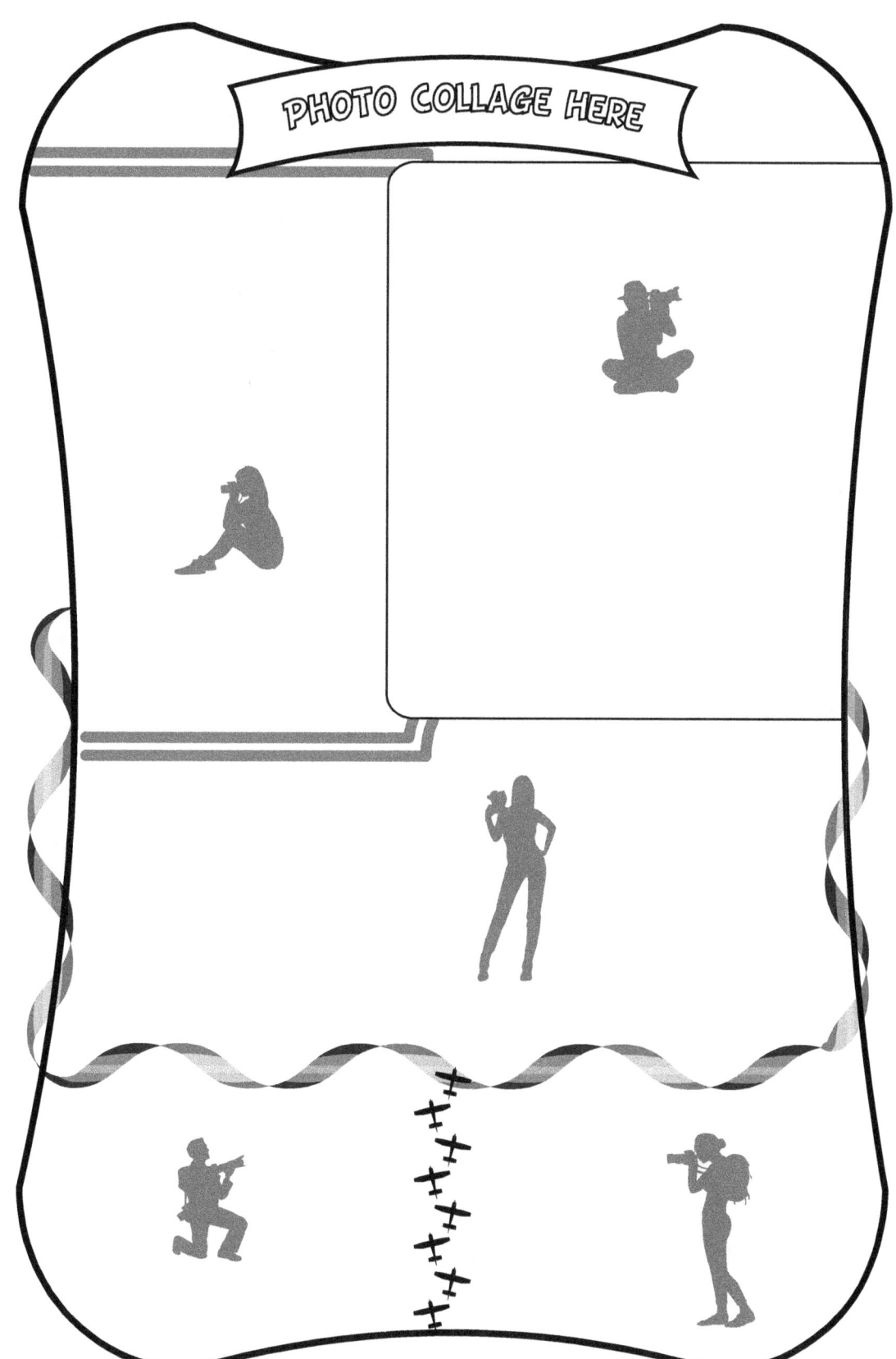

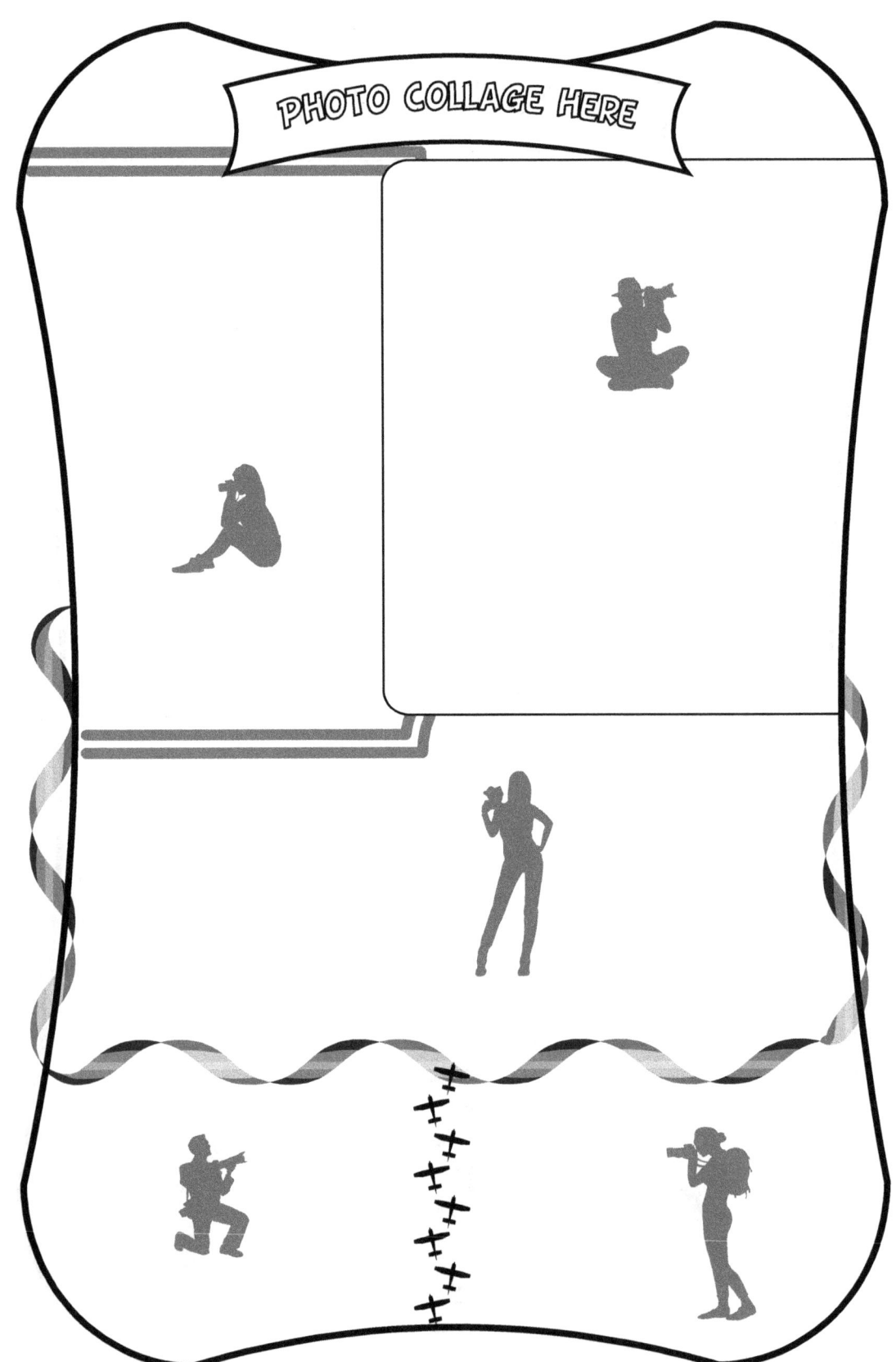

MY TRAVEL JOURNAL

Packing List

- ☐ Visa
- ☐ Passport
- ☐ Tickets
- ☐ ID's
- ☐ Credit Card
- ☐ Camera
- ☐ Chargers
- ☐ Sunglasses
- ☐ Shoes
- ☐ Slippers

Important Reminders

MY TRAVEL JOURNAL

Place to travel :

Hotel Reservation :

Travel Date :

Contact Person/Contact number :

Friends to see / visit :
-
-
-
-
-

Tour Guide :

Contact Person/Contact number :

Places to visti :
-
-
-
-
-
-

photo here

MY TRAVEL JOURNAL

Food Must Try

Shopping list

Food trip photo here

MY TRAVEL JOURNAL

the best part of this travel

unforgettable memories

journal

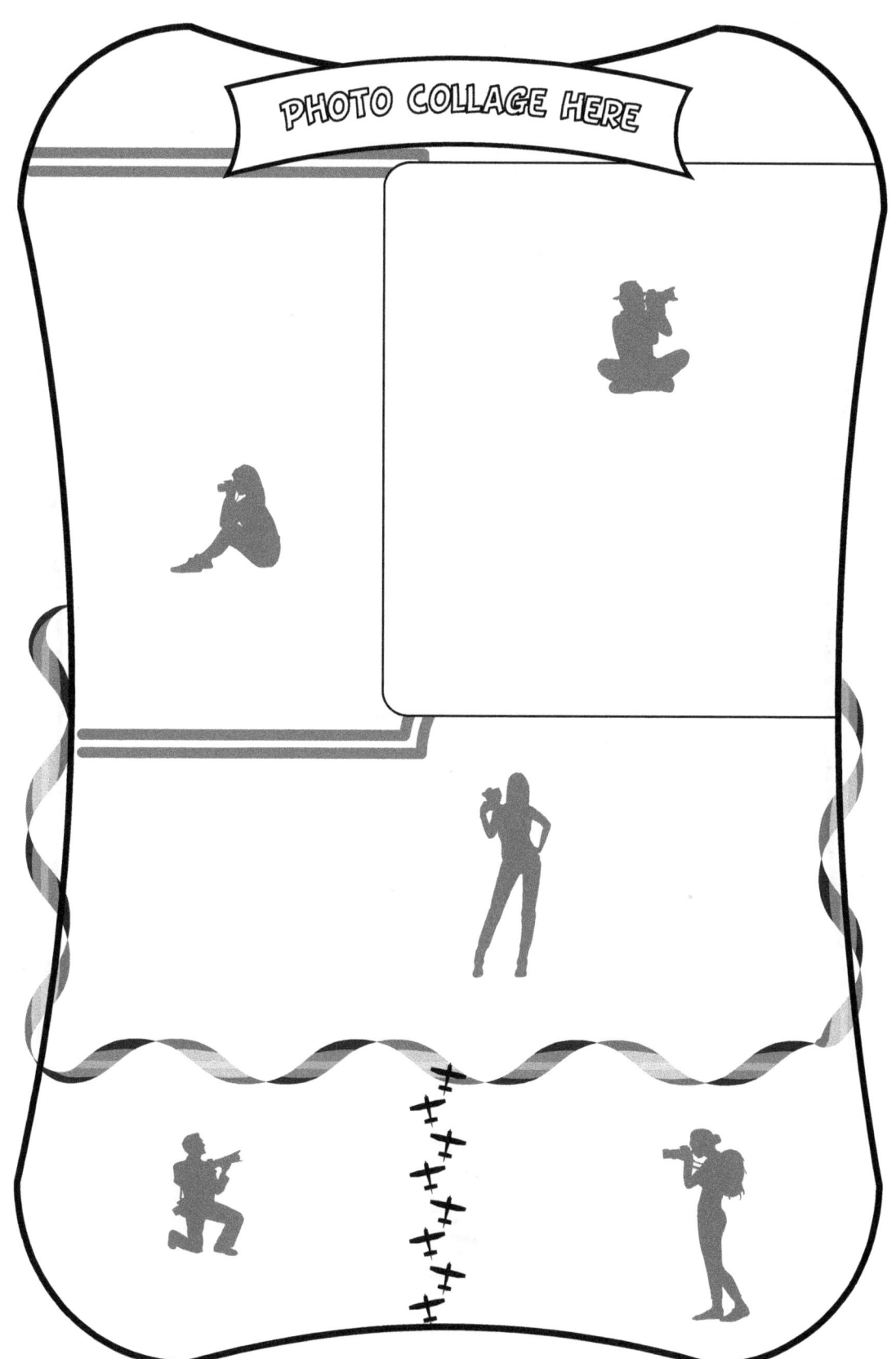

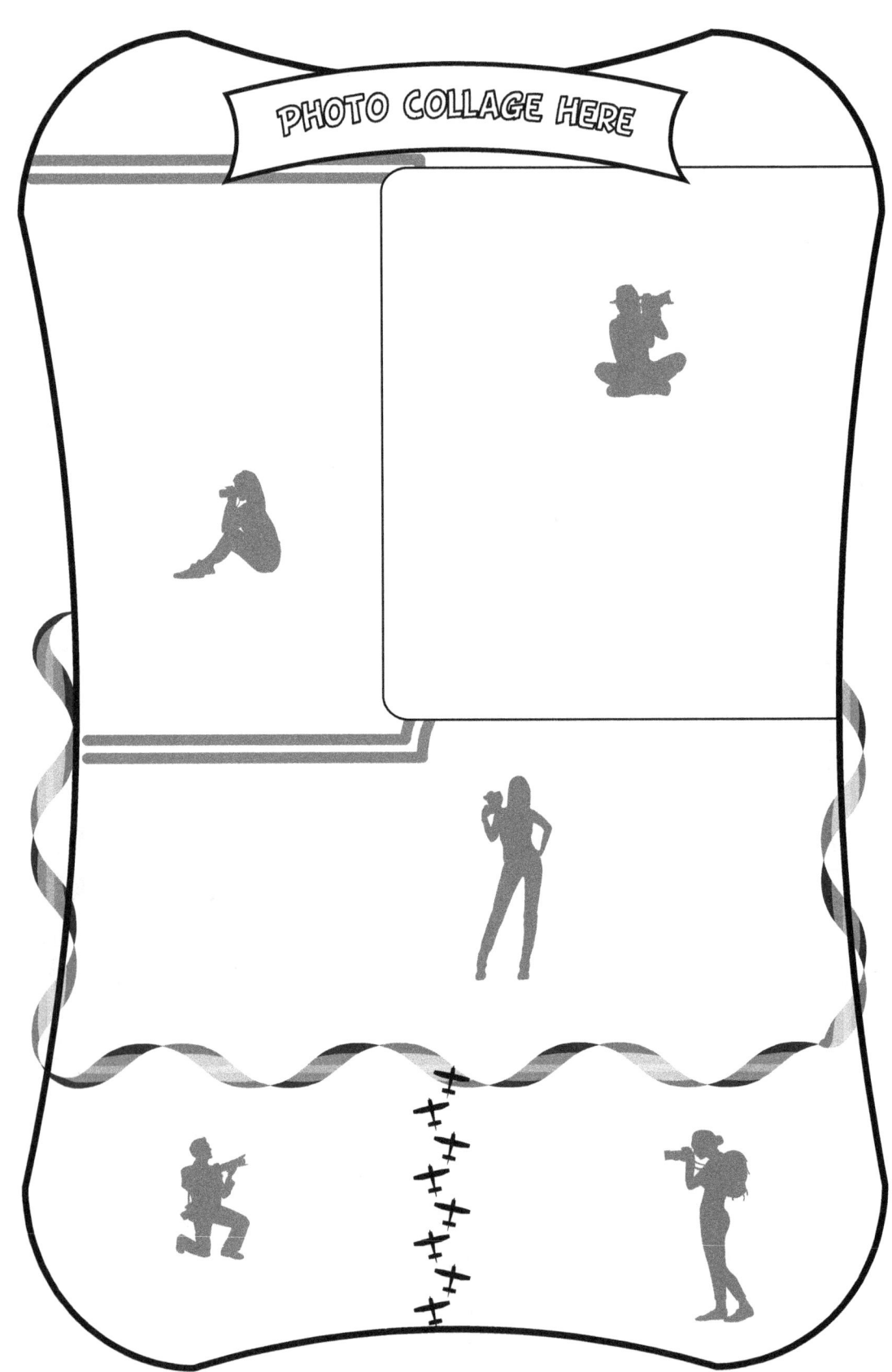

MY TRAVEL JOURNAL

Packing List

- ☐ Visa
- ☐ Passport
- ☐ Tickets
- ☐ ID's
- ☐ Credit Card
- ☐ Camera
- ☐ Chargers
- ☐ Sunglasses
- ☐ Shoes
- ☐ Slippers

Important Reminders

MY TRAVEL JOURNAL

Place to travel :

Hotel Reservation :

Travel Date :

Contact Person/Contact number :

Friends to see / visit :
-
-
-
-
-

Tour Guide :

Contact Person/Contact number :

Places to visti :
-
-
-
-
-

photo here

MY TRAVEL JOURNAL

Food Must Try

Shopping list

Food trip photo here

MY TRAVEL JOURNAL

the best part of this travel

unforgettable memories

journal

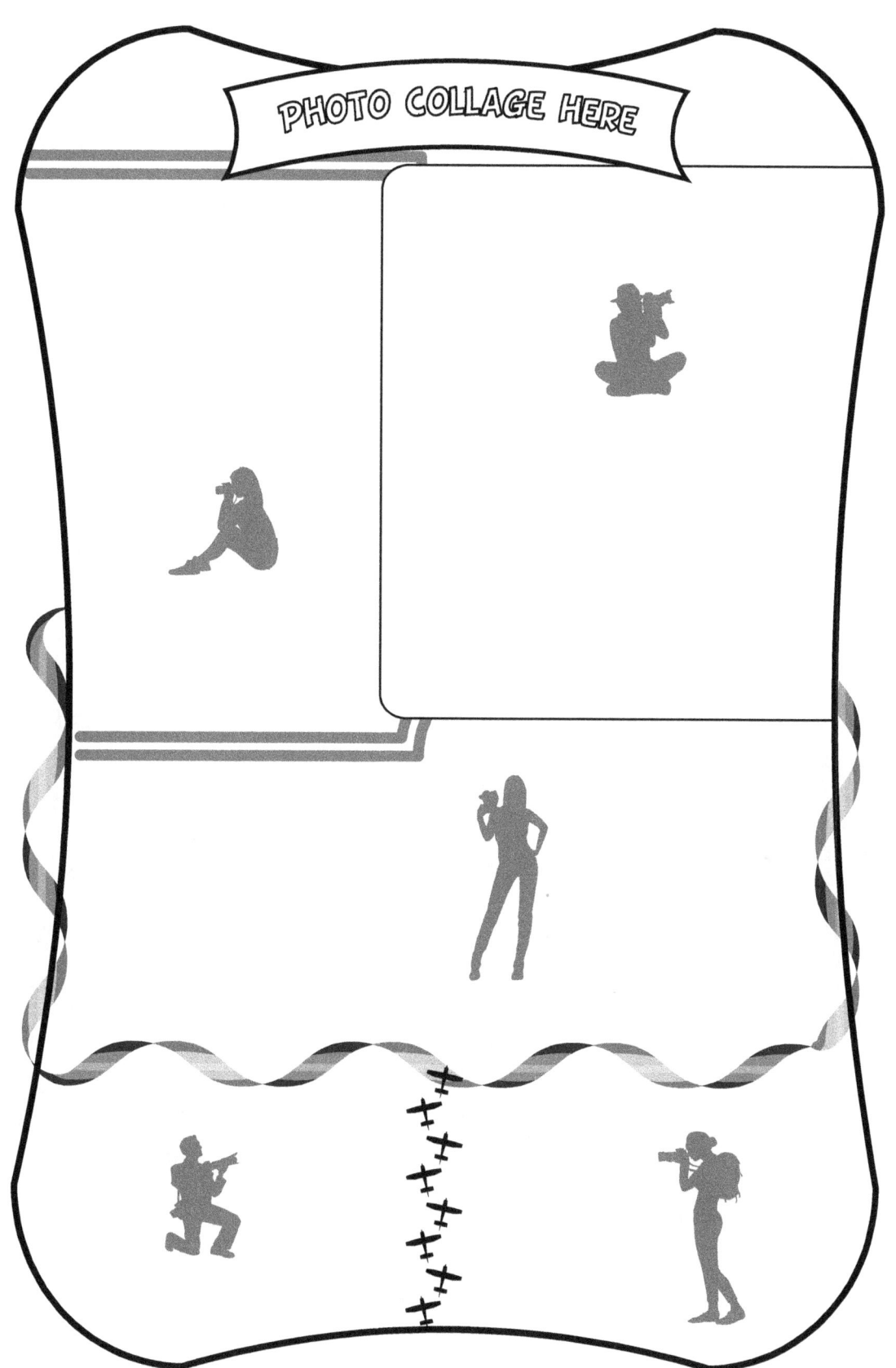

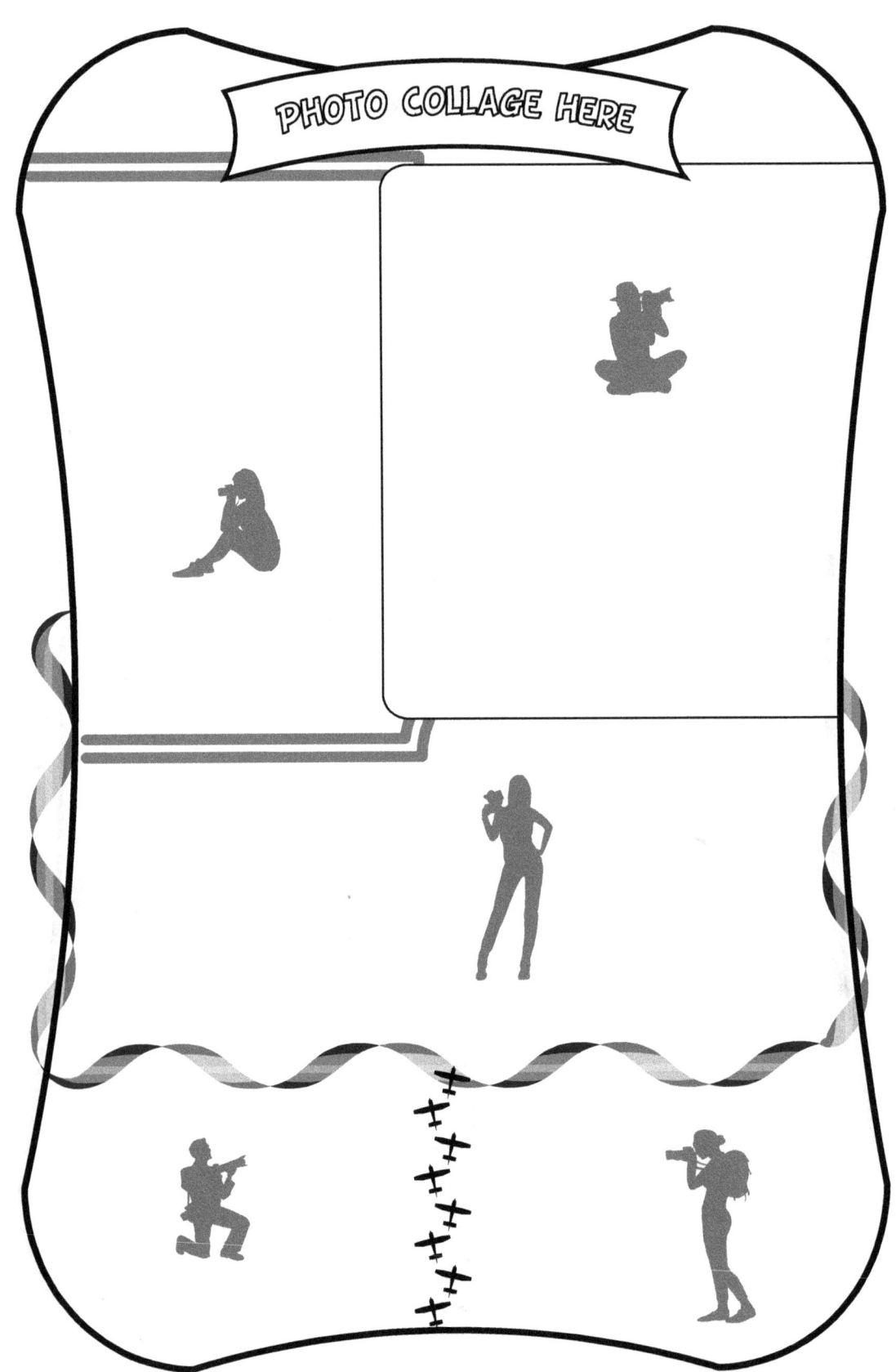

My Travel Journal

Packing List

- ☐ Visa
- ☐ Passport
- ☐ Tickets
- ☐ ID's
- ☐ Credit Card
- ☐ Camera
- ☐ Chargers
- ☐ Sunglasses
- ☐ Shoes
- ☐ Slippers

Important Reminders

MY TRAVEL JOURNAL

Hotel Reservation :

Contact Person/Contact number :

Tour Guide :

Contact Person/Contact number :

Place to travel :

Travel Date :

Friends to see / visit :
-
-
-
-
-

Places to visti :
-
-
-
-
-
-

photo here

MY
TRAVEL JOURNAL

Shopping list

Food Must Try

Food trip photo here

MY TRAVEL JOURNAL

the best part of this travel

unforgettable memories

journal

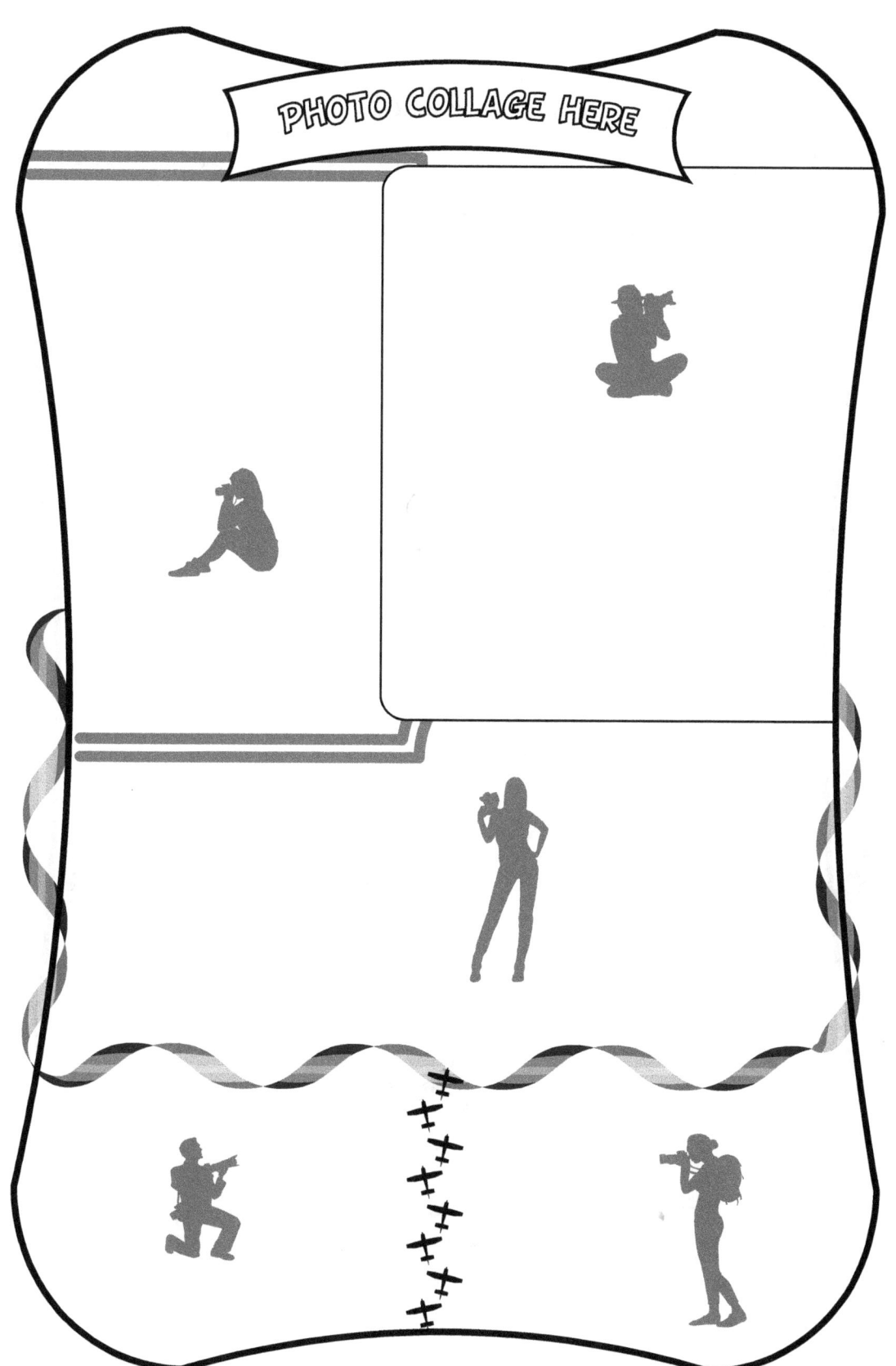

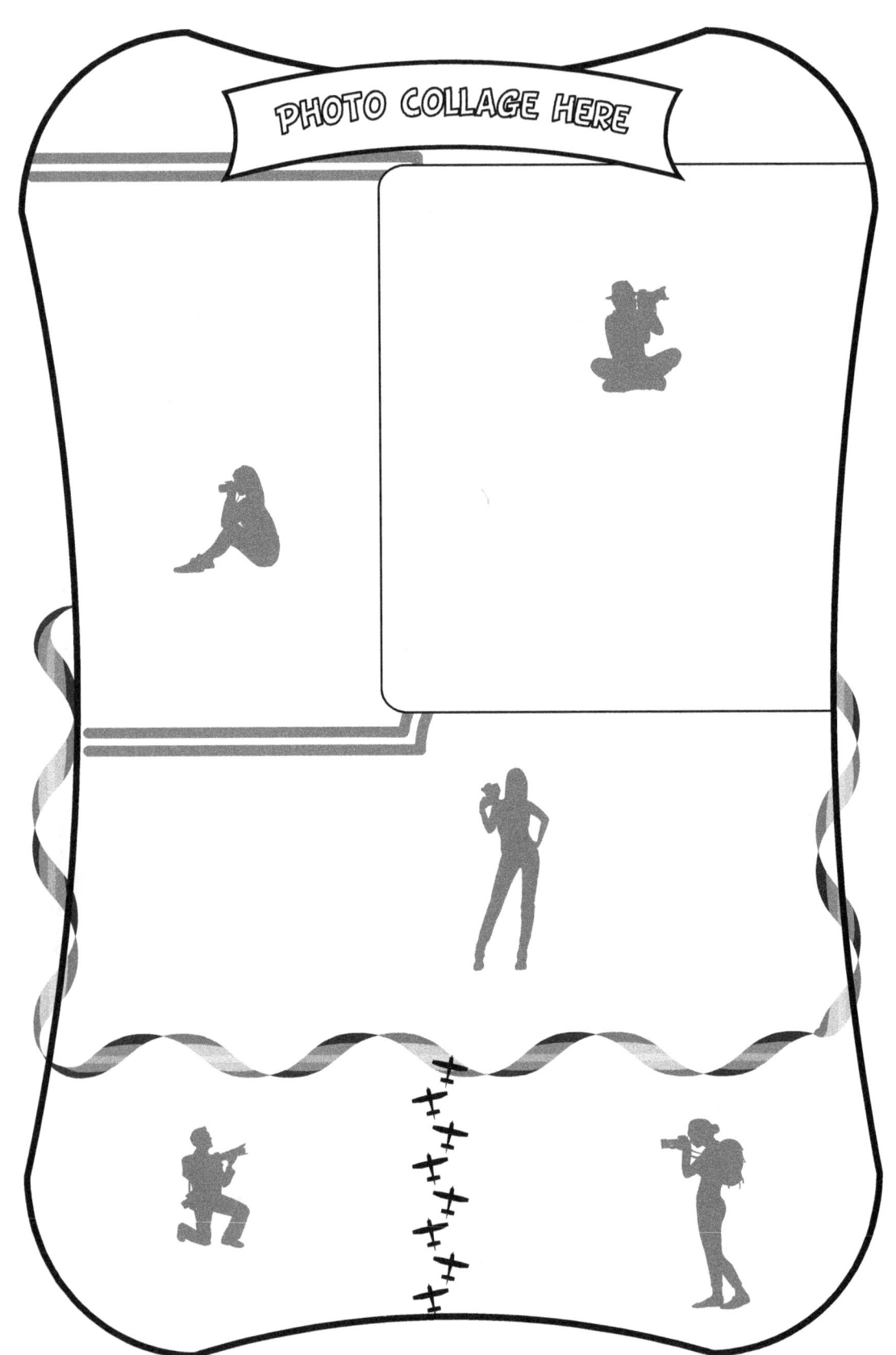

MY TRAVEL JOURNAL

Packing List

- ☐ Visa
- ☐ Passport
- ☐ Tickets
- ☐ ID's
- ☐ Credit Card
- ☐ Camera
- ☐ Chargers
- ☐ Sunglasses
- ☐ Shoes
- ☐ Slippers

Important Reminders

MY TRAVEL JOURNAL

Place to travel :

Hotel Reservation :

Travel Date :

Contact Person/Contact number :

Tour Guide :

Friends to see / visit :
-
-
-
-
-

Contact Person/Contact number :

Places to visti :
-
-
-
-
-
-

photo here

MY TRAVEL JOURNAL

Shopping list

Food Must Try

Food trip photo here

MY TRAVEL JOURNAL

the best part of this travel

unforgettable memories

journal

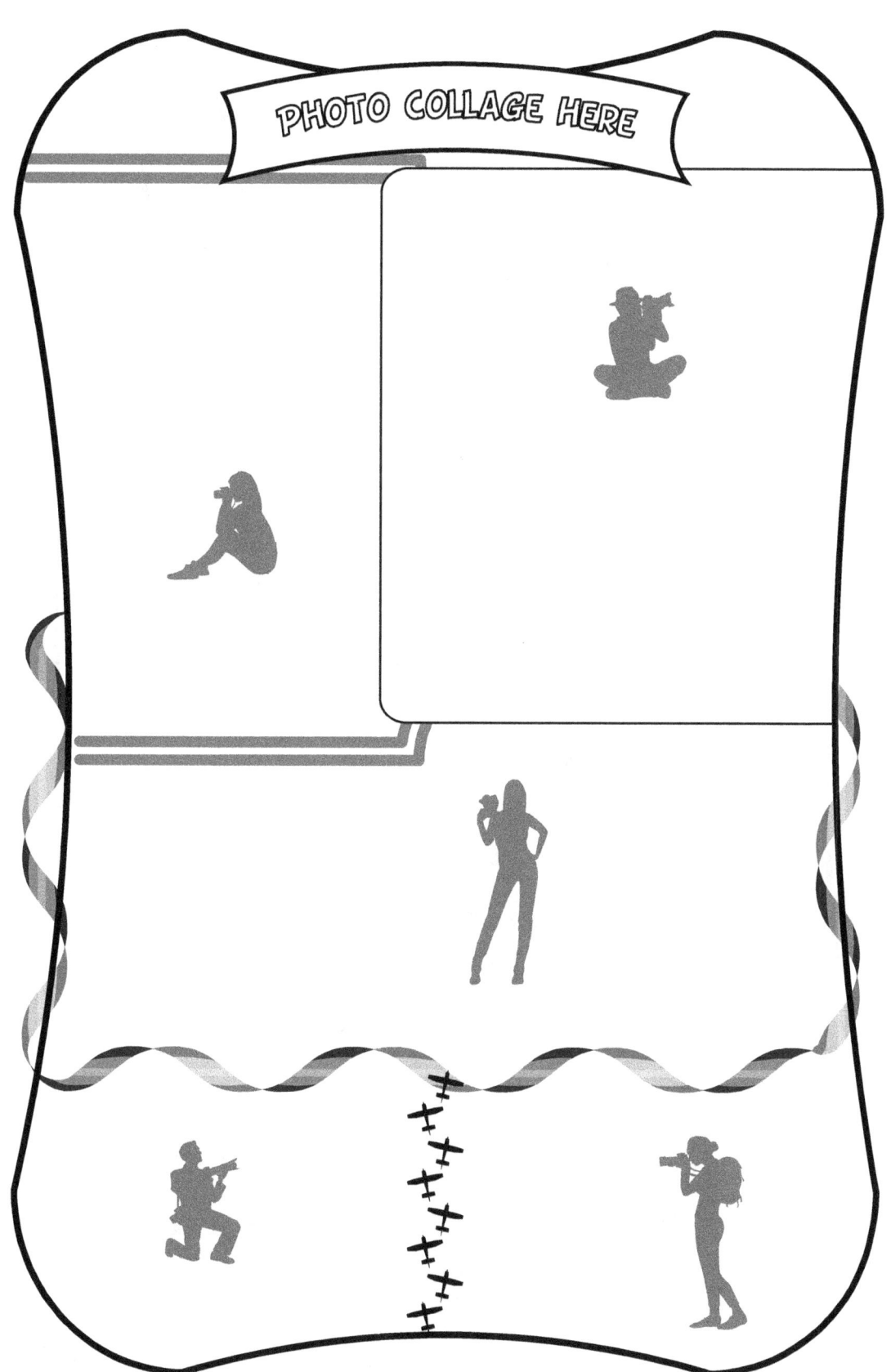

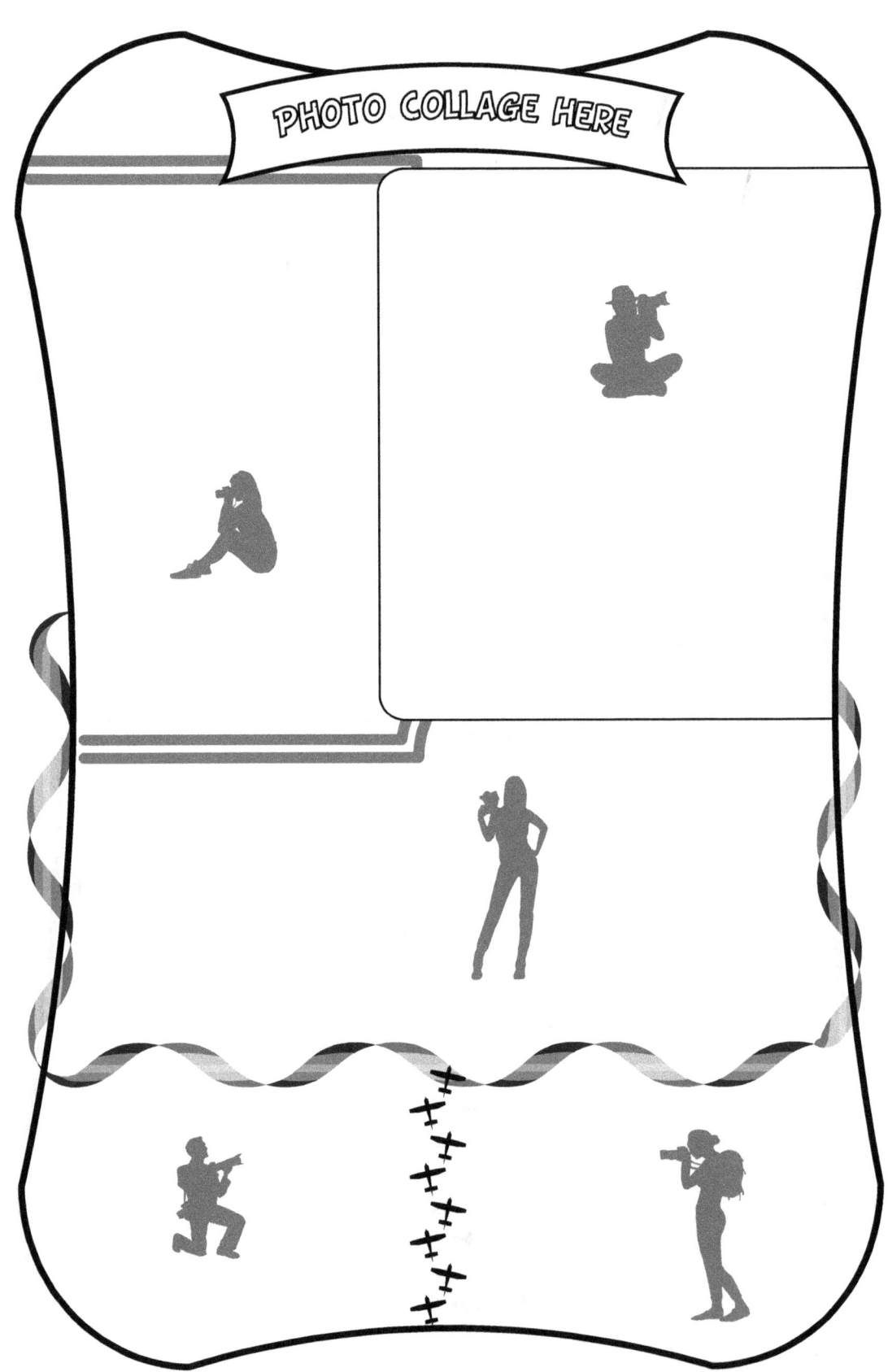

MY TRAVEL JOURNAL

Packing List

- ☐ Visa
- ☐ Passport
- ☐ Tickets
- ☐ ID's
- ☐ Credit Card
- ☐ Camera
- ☐ Chargers
- ☐ Sunglasses
- ☐ Shoes
- ☐ Slippers

Important Reminders

MY TRAVEL JOURNAL

Place to travel :

Hotel Reservation :

Travel Date :

Contact Person/Contact number :

Tour Guide :

Friends to see / visit :
-
-
-
-
-

Contact Person/Contact number :

Places to visti :
-
-
-
-
-

photo here

MY TRAVEL JOURNAL

Shopping list

Food trip photo here

MY TRAVEL JOURNAL

the best part of this travel

unforgettable memories

journal

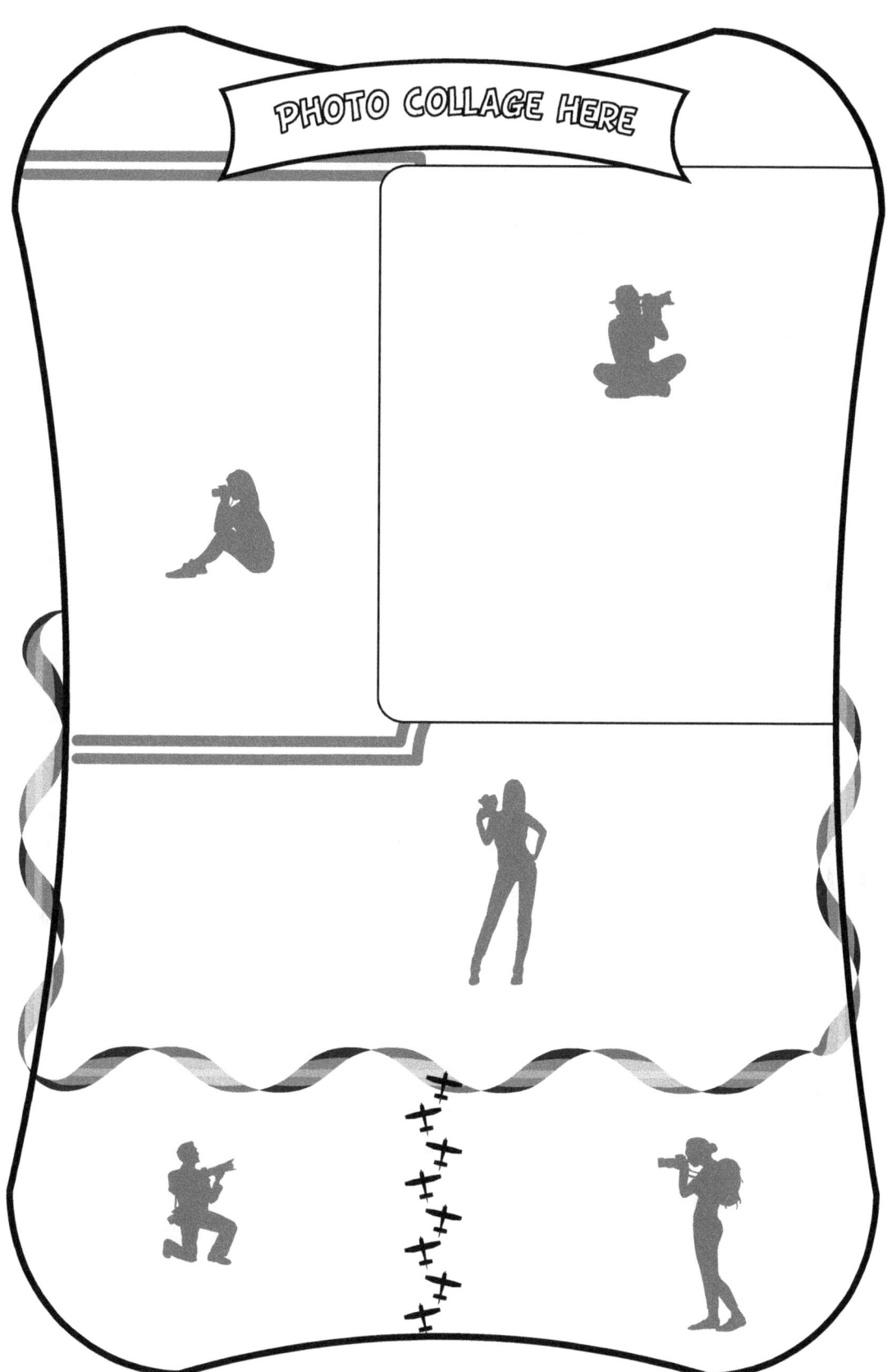

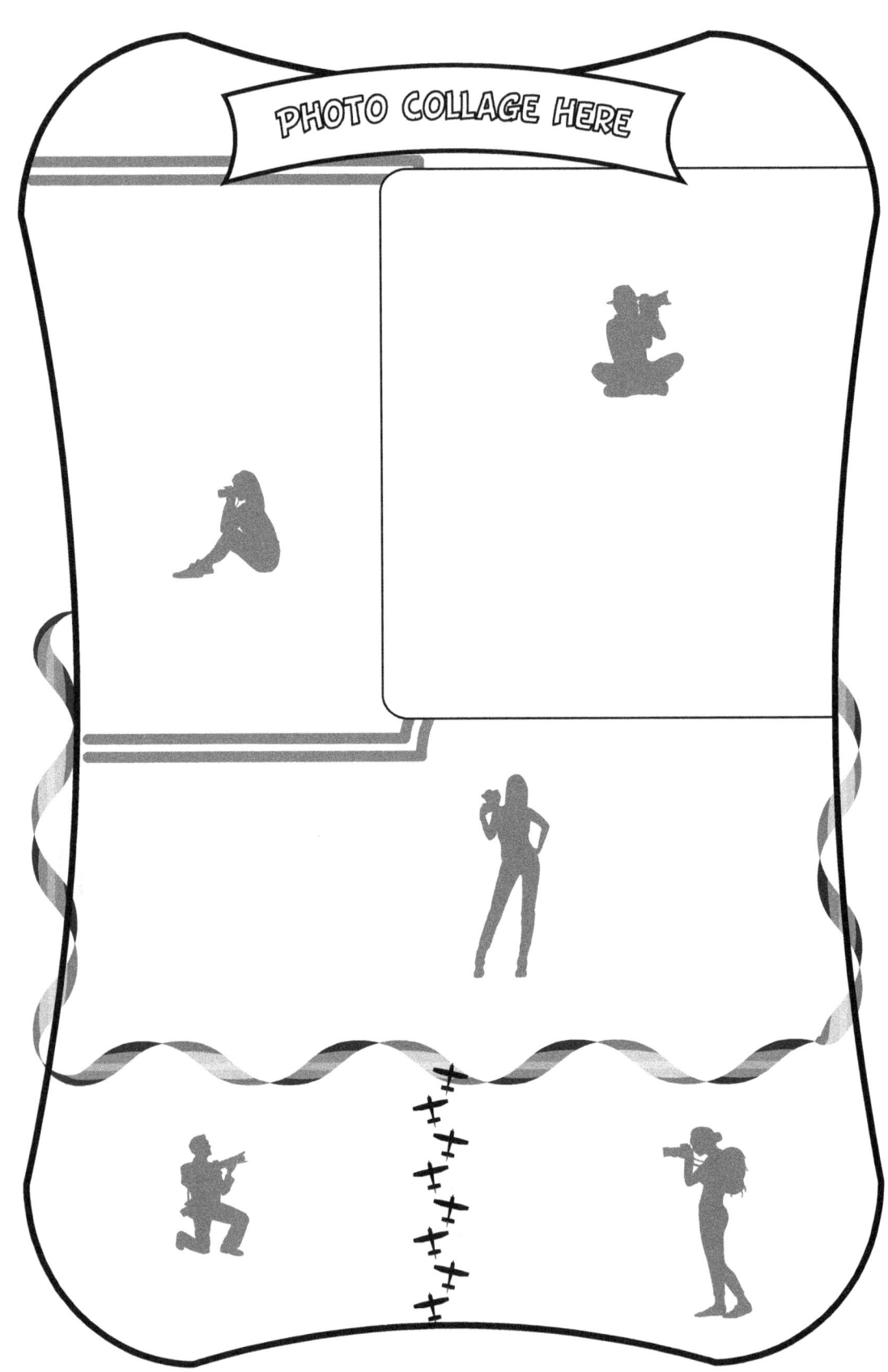

MY TRAVEL JOURNAL

Packing List

- ☐ Visa
- ☐ Passport
- ☐ Tickets
- ☐ ID's
- ☐ Credit Card
- ☐ Camera
- ☐ Chargers
- ☐ Sunglasses
- ☐ Shoes
- ☐ Slippers

Important Reminders

MY TRAVEL JOURNAL

Hotel Reservation :

Place to travel :

Travel Date :

Contact Person/Contact number :

Tour Guide :

Friends to see / visit :
-
-
-
-
-

Contact Person/Contact number :

Places to visti :
-
-
-
-
-
-

photo here

MY TRAVEL JOURNAL

Food Must Try

Shopping list

Food trip photo here

MY TRAVEL JOURNAL

the best part of this travel

unforgettable memories

journal

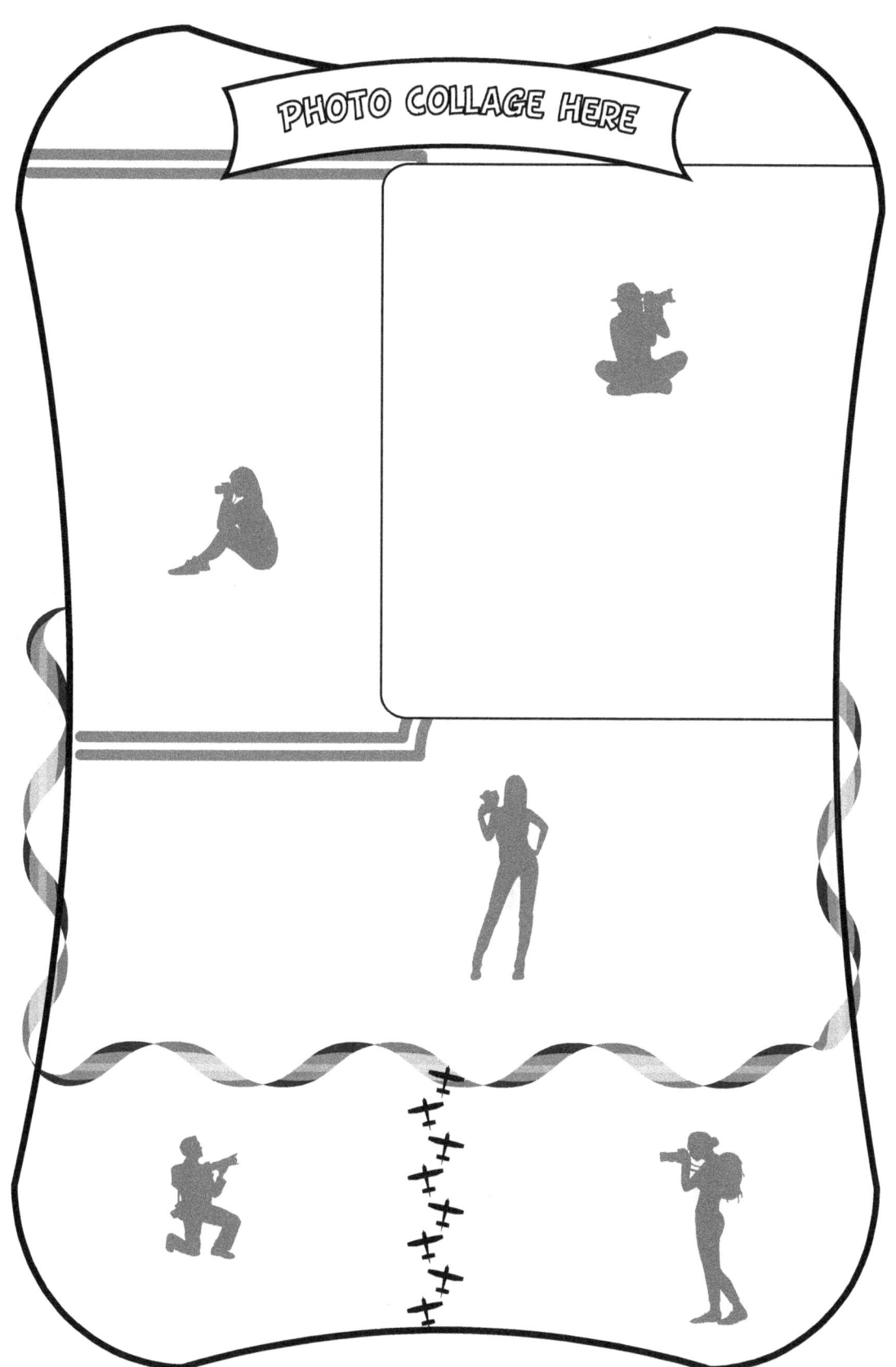

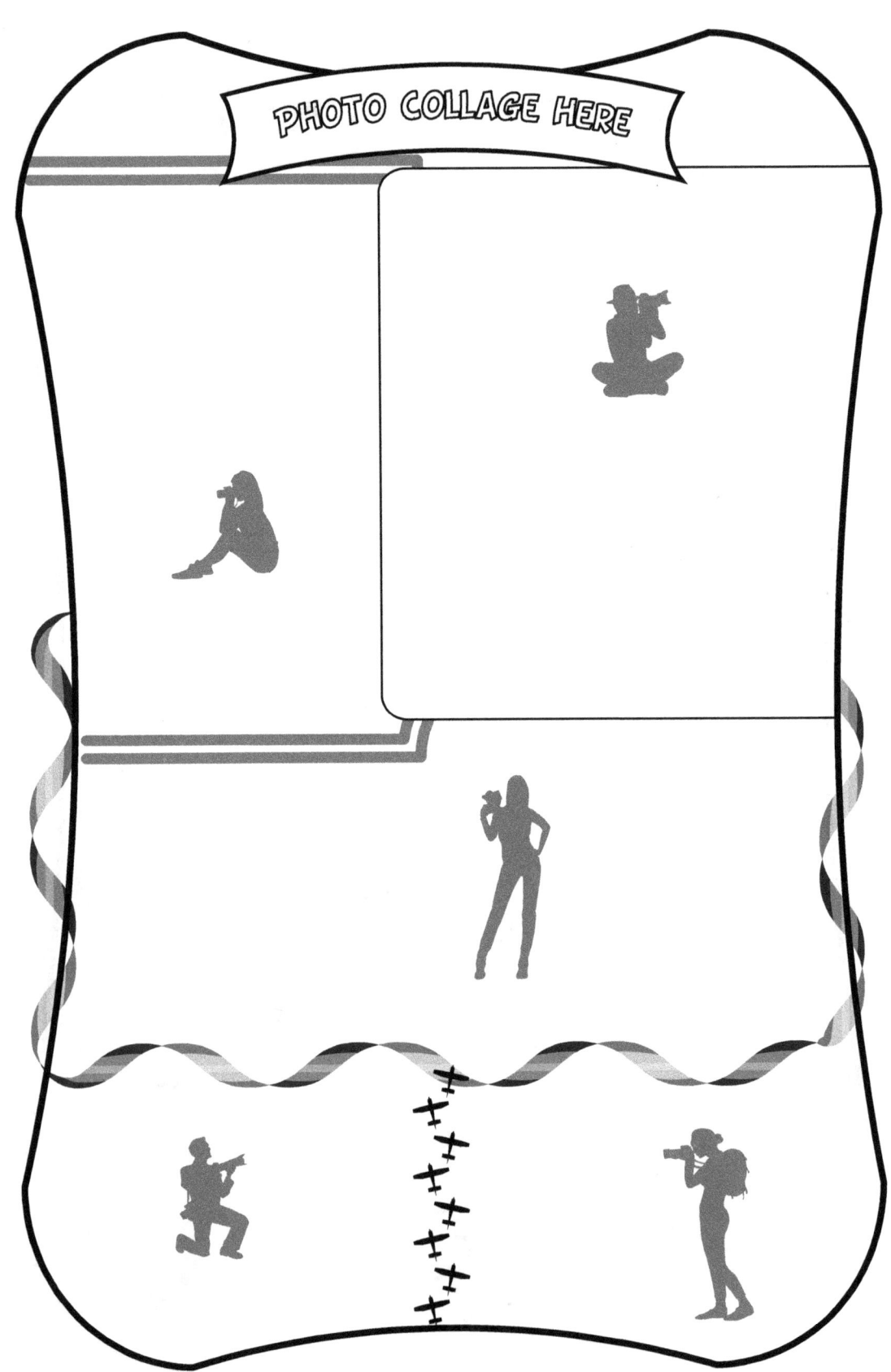

MY TRAVEL JOURNAL

Packing List

- ☐ Visa
- ☐ Passport
- ☐ Tickets
- ☐ ID's
- ☐ Credit Card
- ☐ Camera
- ☐ Chargers
- ☐ Sunglasses
- ☐ Shoes
- ☐ Slippers

Important Reminders

MY TRAVEL JOURNAL

Place to travel :

Hotel Reservation :

Travel Date :

Contact Person/Contact number :

Friends to see / visit :
-
-
-
-
-

Tour Guide :

Contact Person/Contact number :

Places to visti :
-
-
-
-
-
-

photo here

MY TRAVEL JOURNAL

Food Must Try

Shopping list

Food trip photo here

MY TRAVEL JOURNAL

the best part of this travel

unforgettable memories

journal

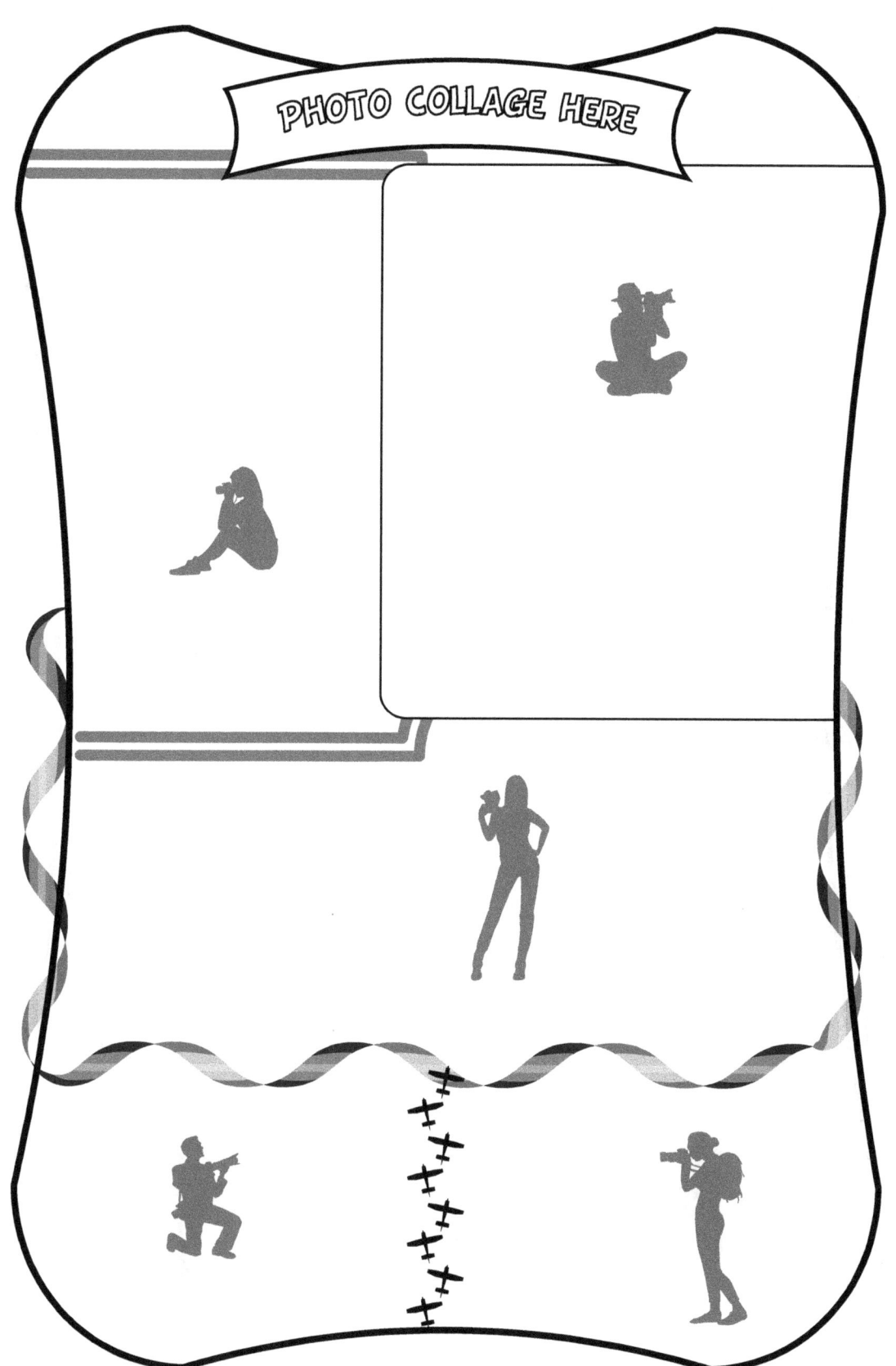

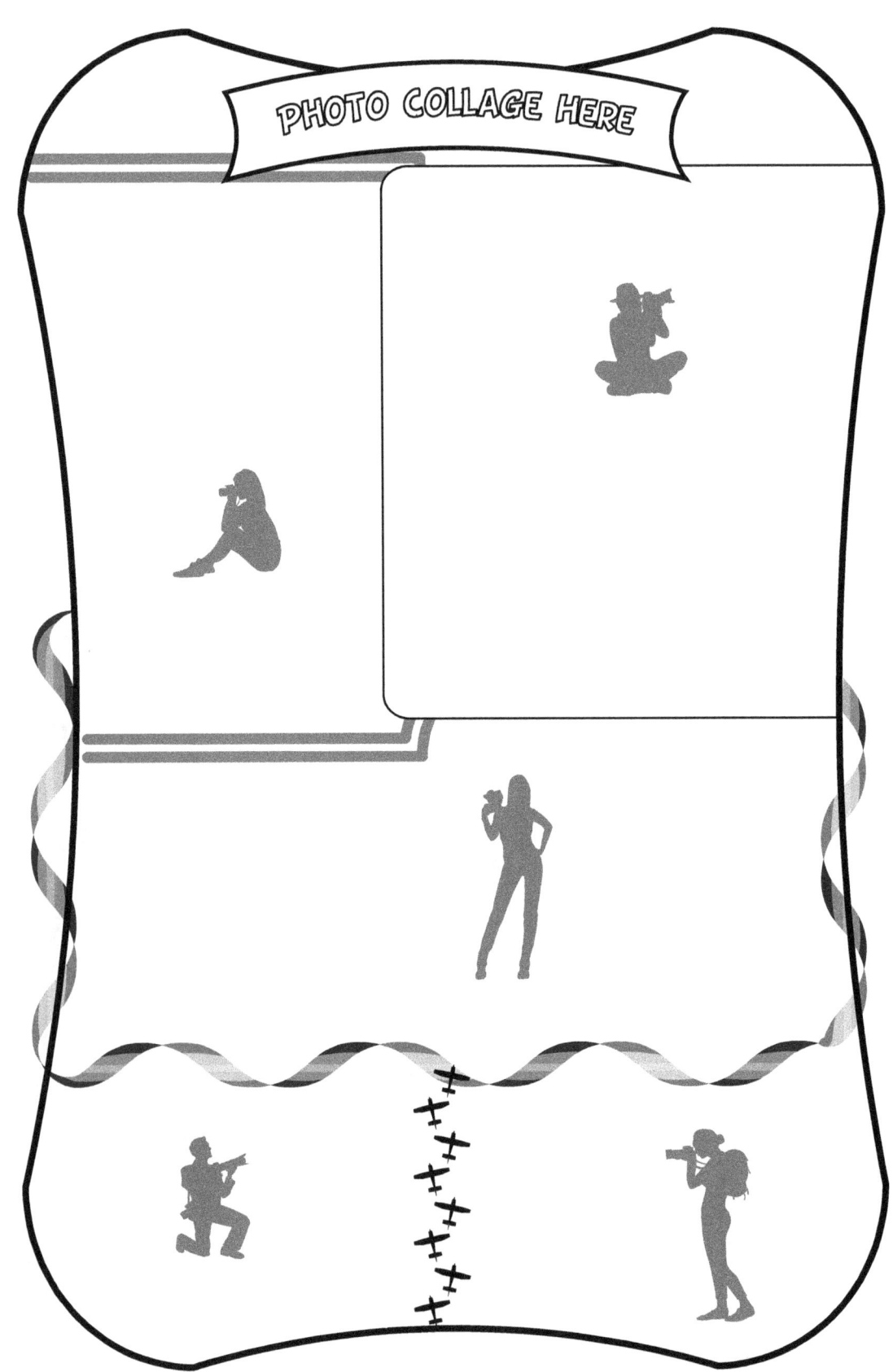

MY TRAVEL JOURNAL

Packing List

- ☐ Visa
- ☐ Passport
- ☐ Tickets
- ☐ ID's
- ☐ Credit Card
- ☐ Camera
- ☐ Chargers
- ☐ Sunglasses
- ☐ Shoes
- ☐ Slippers

Important Reminders

MY TRAVEL JOURNAL

Place to travel :

Hotel Reservation :

Travel Date :

Contact Person/Contact number :

Friends to see / visit :
-
-
-
-
-

Tour Guide :

Contact Person/Contact number :

Places to visti :
-
-
-
-
-
-

photo here

MY
TRAVEL JOURNAL

Food Must Try

Shopping list

Food trip photo here

MY TRAVEL JOURNAL

the best part of this travel

unforgettable memories

journal

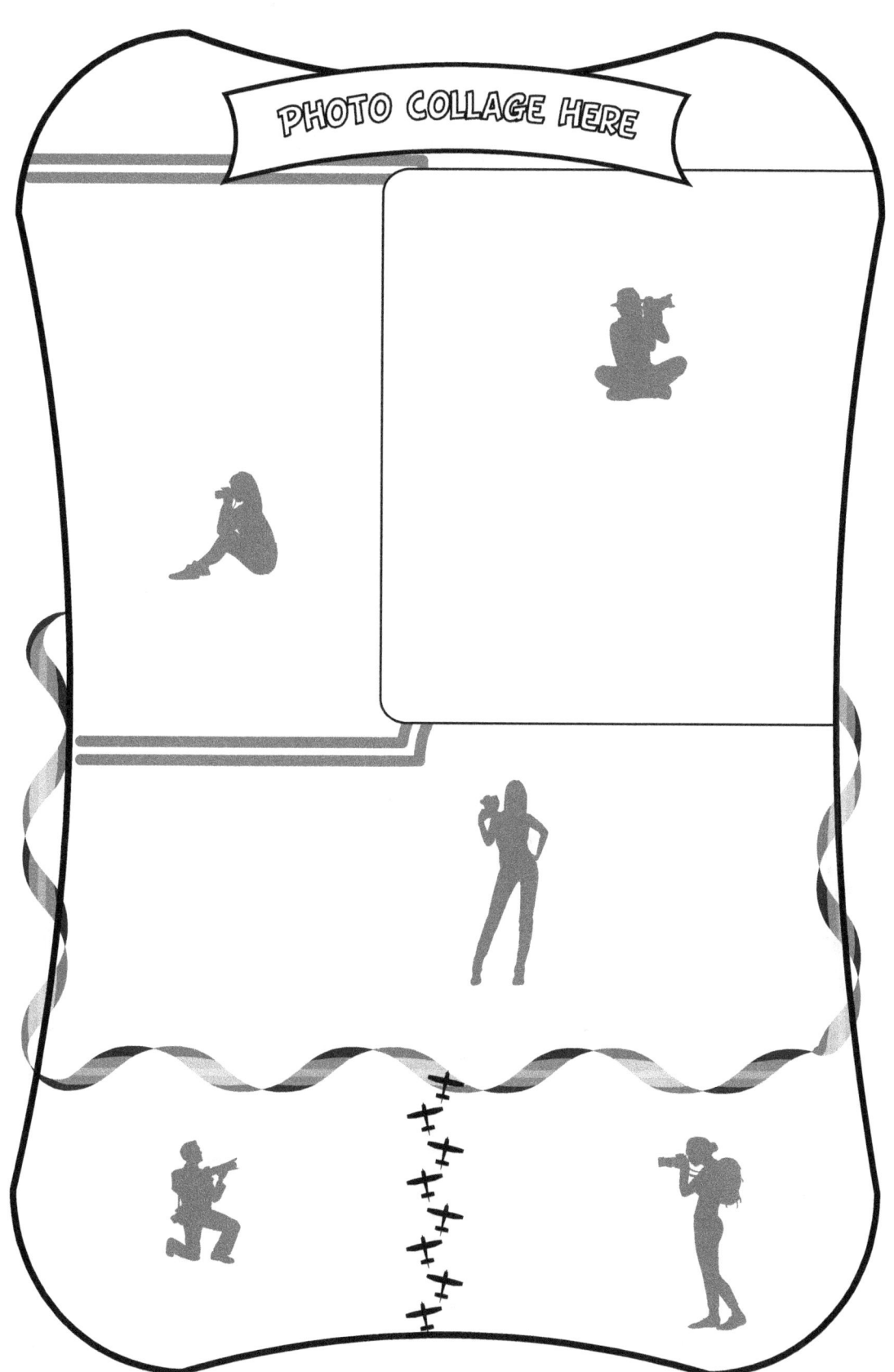

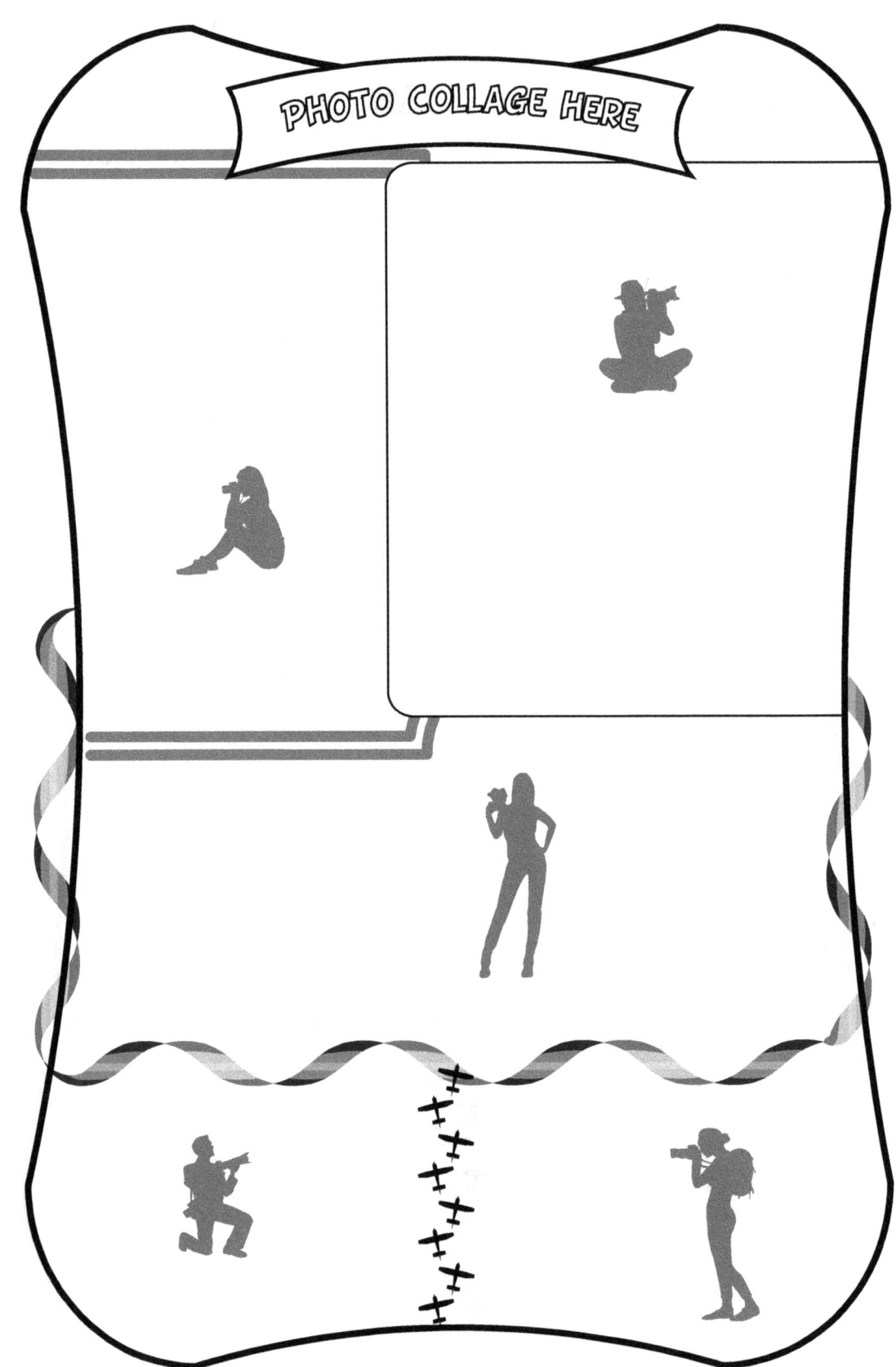

MY TRAVEL JOURNAL

Packing List

- ☐ Visa
- ☐ Passport
- ☐ Tickets
- ☐ ID's
- ☐ Credit Card
- ☐ Camera
- ☐ Chargers
- ☐ Sunglasses
- ☐ Shoes
- ☐ Slippers

Important Reminders

MY TRAVEL JOURNAL

Place to travel :

Hotel Reservation :

Travel Date :

Contact Person/Contact number :

Friends to see / visit :
-
-
-
-
-

Tour Guide :

Contact Person/Contact number :

Places to visti :
-
-
-
-
-
-

photo here

MY TRAVEL JOURNAL

Food Must Try

Shopping list

Food trip photo here

MY TRAVEL JOURNAL

the best part of this travel

unforgettable memories

journal

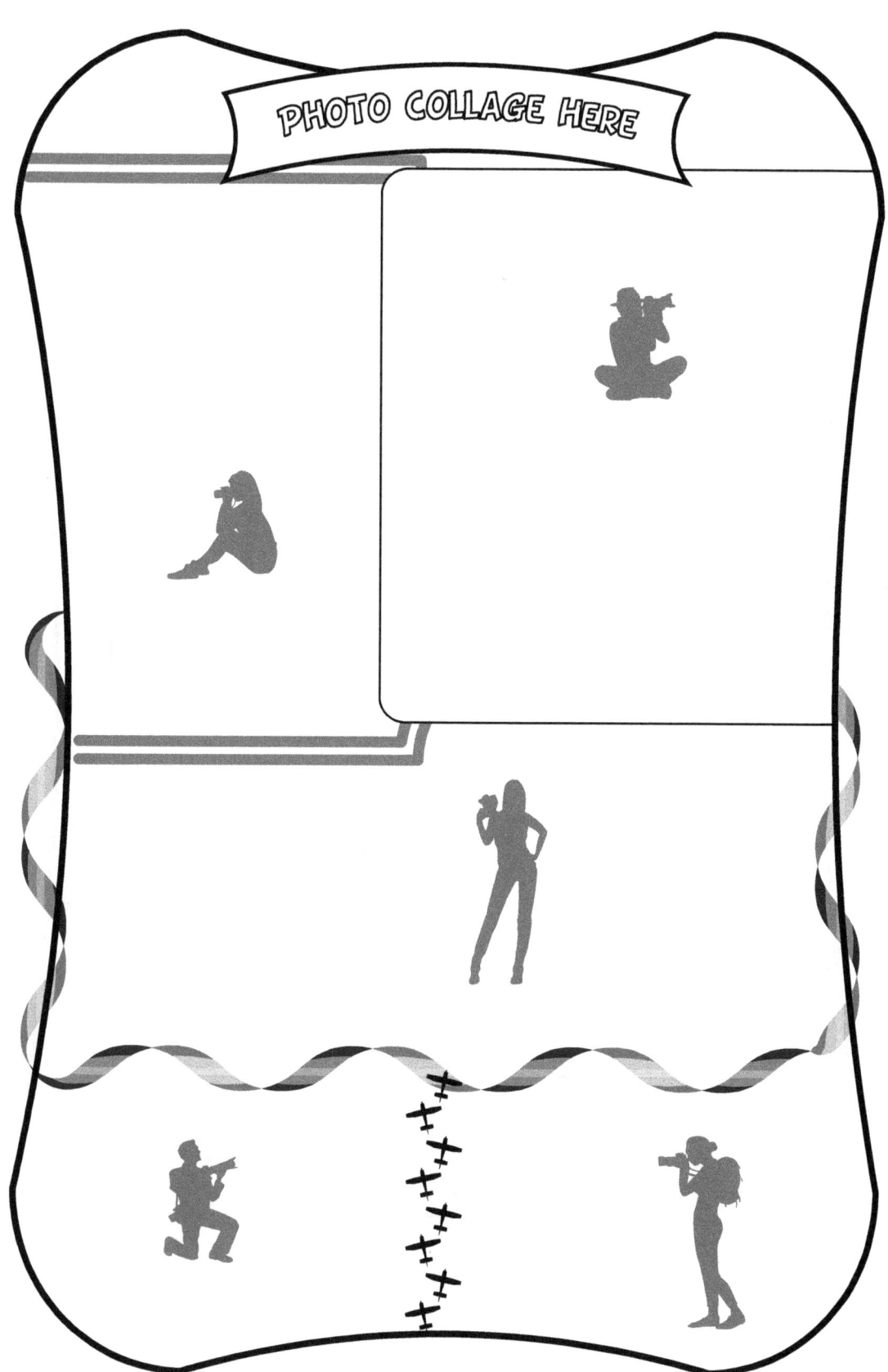

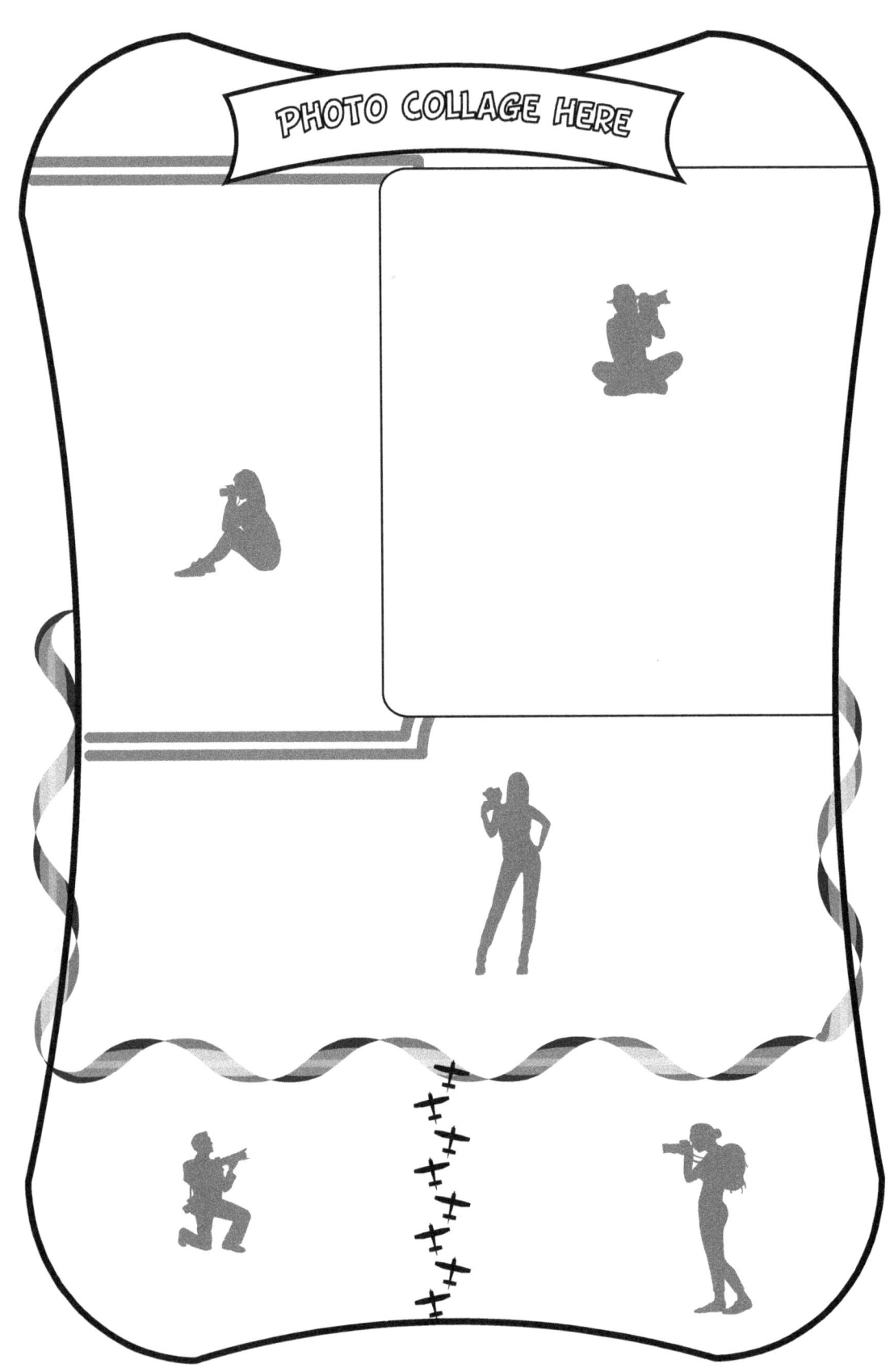

MY TRAVEL JOURNAL

Packing List

- ☐ Visa
- ☐ Passport
- ☐ Tickets
- ☐ ID's
- ☐ Credit Card
- ☐ Camera
- ☐ Chargers
- ☐ Sunglasses
- ☐ Shoes
- ☐ Slippers

Important Reminders

MY TRAVEL JOURNAL

Place to travel :

Hotel Reservation :

Travel Date :

Contact Person/Contact number :

Tour Guide :

Friends to see / visit :
-
-
-
-
-

Contact Person/Contact number :

Places to visti :
-
-
-
-
-
-

photo here

MY TRAVEL JOURNAL

Shopping list

Food Must Try

Food trip photo here

MY TRAVEL JOURNAL

the best part of this travel

unforgettable memories

journal

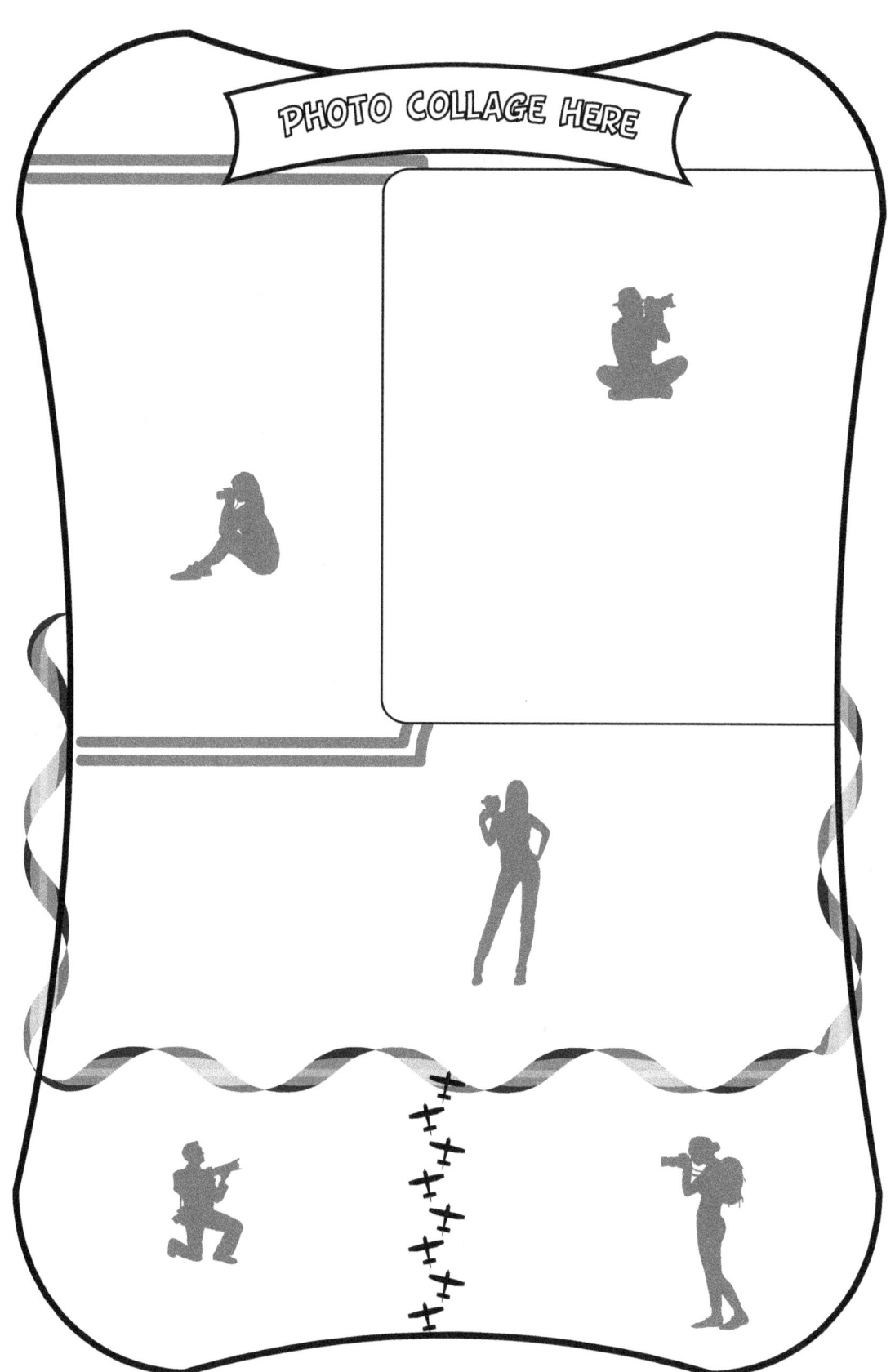

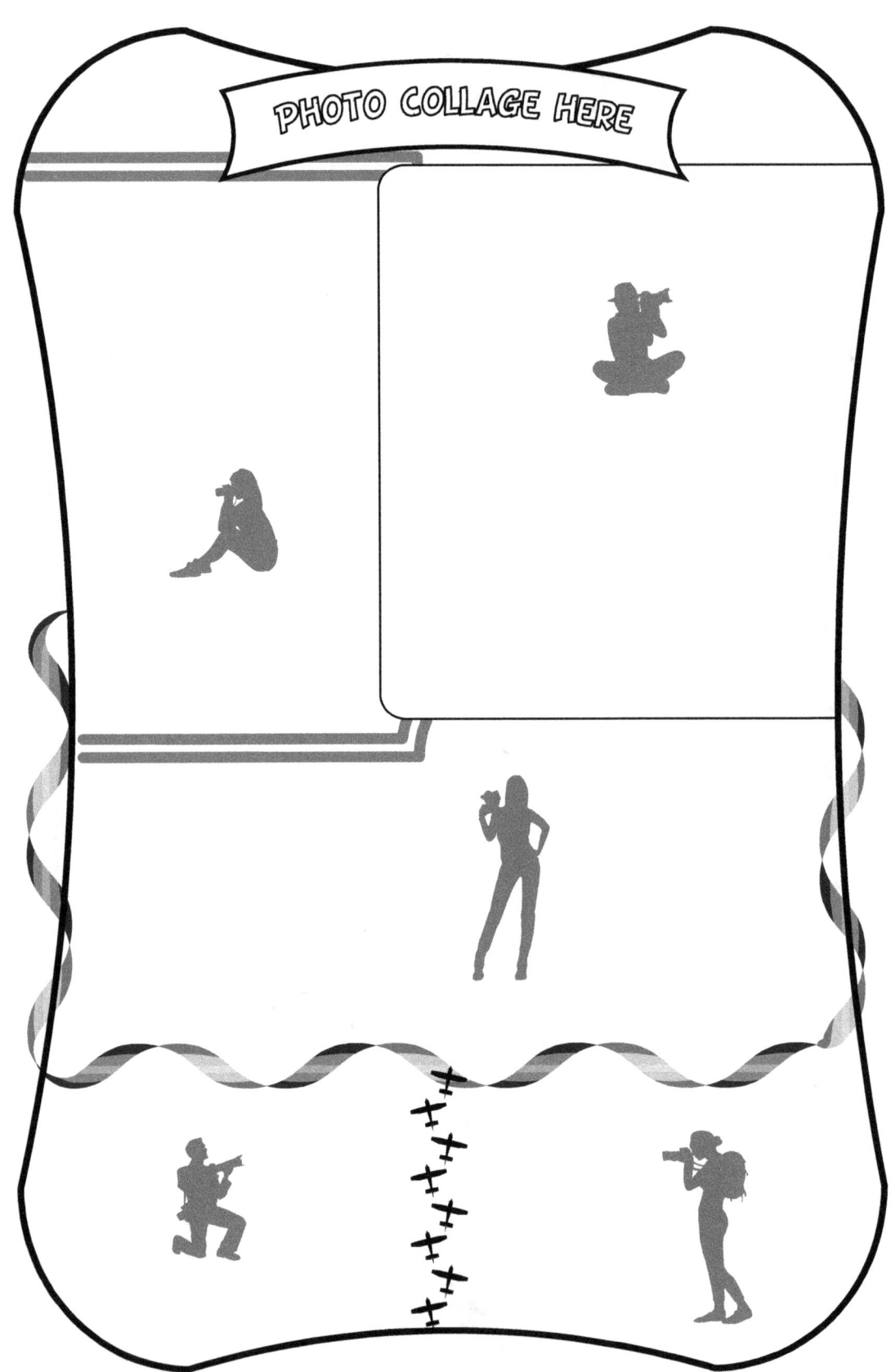

My Travel Journal

Packing List

- ☐ Visa
- ☐ Passport
- ☐ Tickets
- ☐ ID's
- ☐ Credit Card
- ☐ Camera
- ☐ Chargers
- ☐ Sunglasses
- ☐ Shoes
- ☐ Slippers

Important Reminders

MY TRAVEL JOURNAL

Place to travel :

Hotel Reservation :

Travel Date :

Contact Person/Contact number :

Friends to see / visit :
-
-
-
-

Tour Guide :

Contact Person/Contact number :

Places to visti :
-
-
-
-
-

photo here

MY TRAVEL JOURNAL

Food Must Try

Shopping list

Food trip photo here

MY TRAVEL JOURNAL

the best part of this travel

unforgettable memories

journal

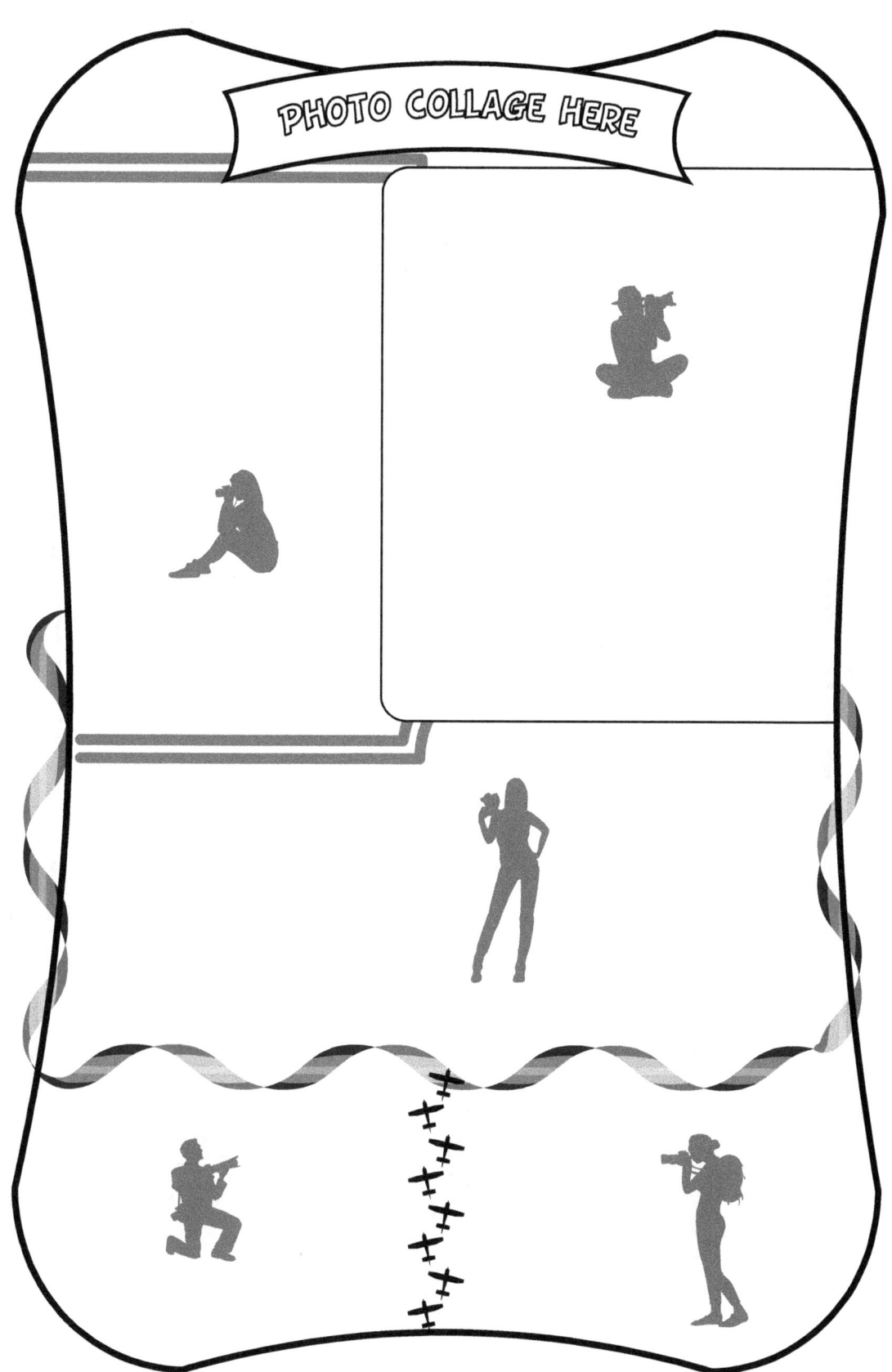

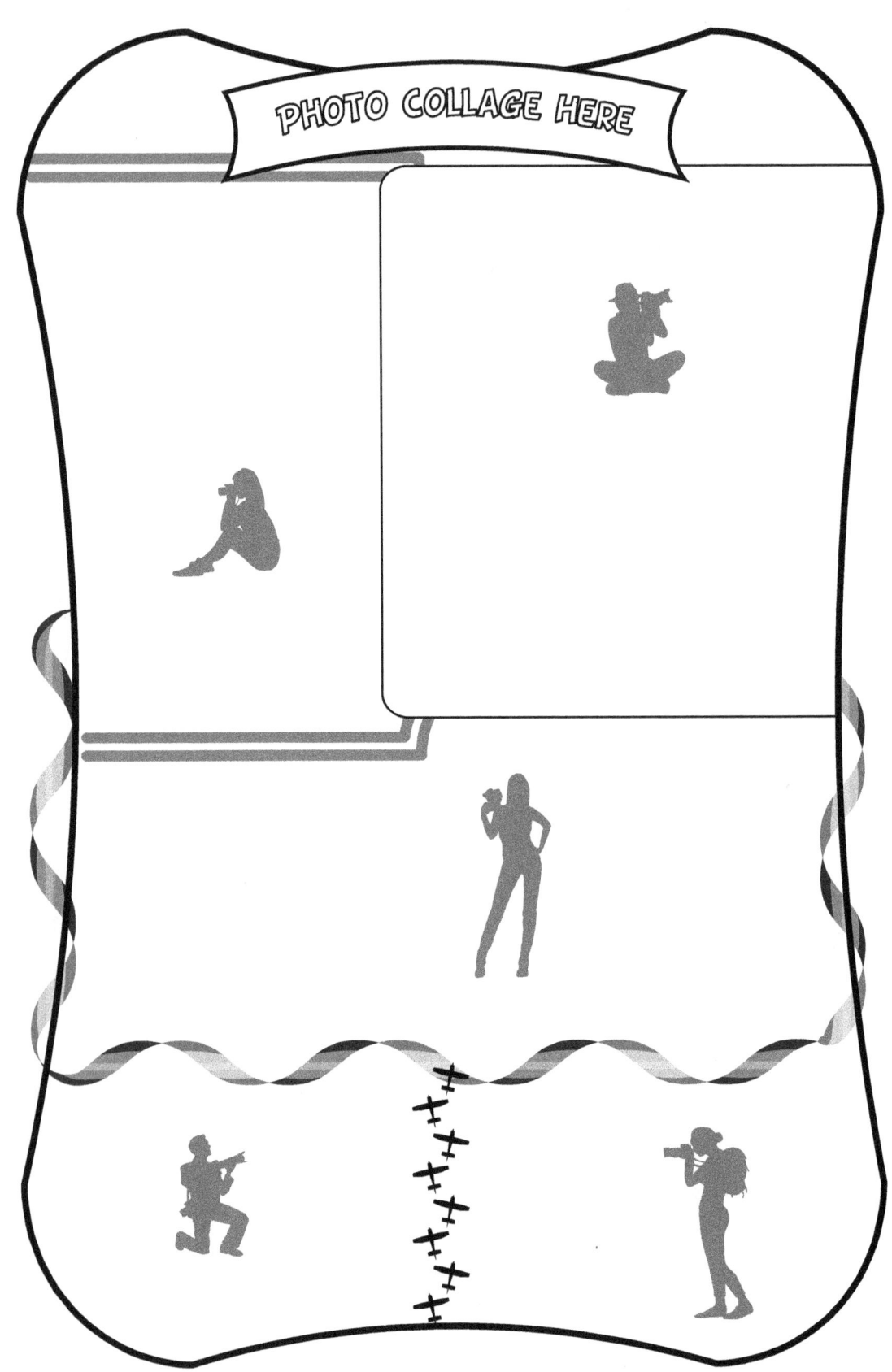

MY TRAVEL JOURNAL

Packing List

- ☐ Visa
- ☐ Passport
- ☐ Tickets
- ☐ ID's
- ☐ Credit Card
- ☐ Camera
- ☐ Chargers
- ☐ Sunglasses
- ☐ Shoes
- ☐ Slippers

Important Reminders

MY TRAVEL JOURNAL

Place to travel :

Hotel Reservation :

Travel Date :

Contact Person/Contact number :

Tour Guide :

Friends to see / visit :

-
-
-
-

Contact Person/Contact number :

Places to visti :

-
-
-
-
-

photo here

MY TRAVEL JOURNAL

Food Must Try

Shopping list

Food trip photo here

MY TRAVEL JOURNAL

the best part of this travel

unforgettable memories

journal

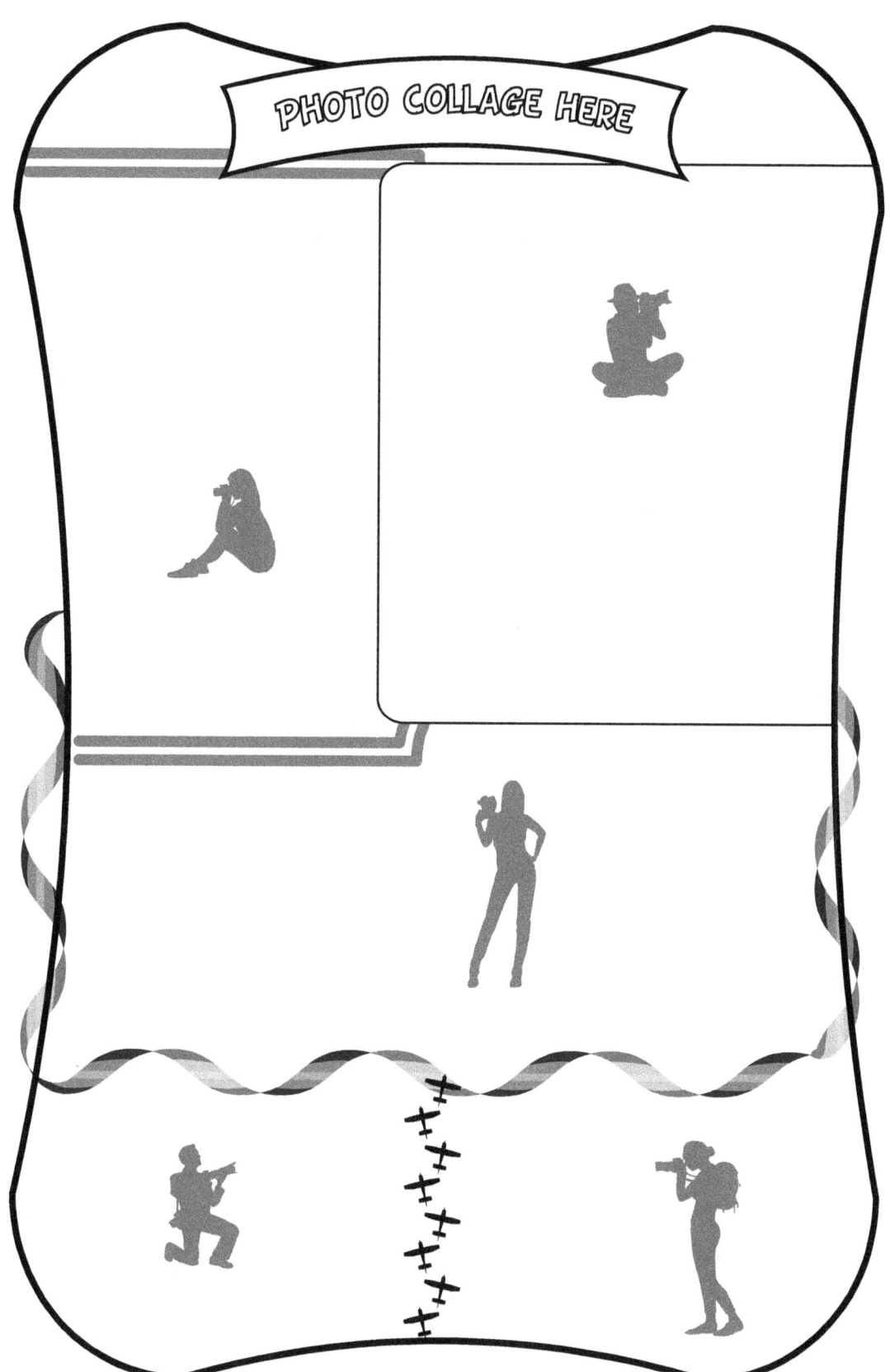

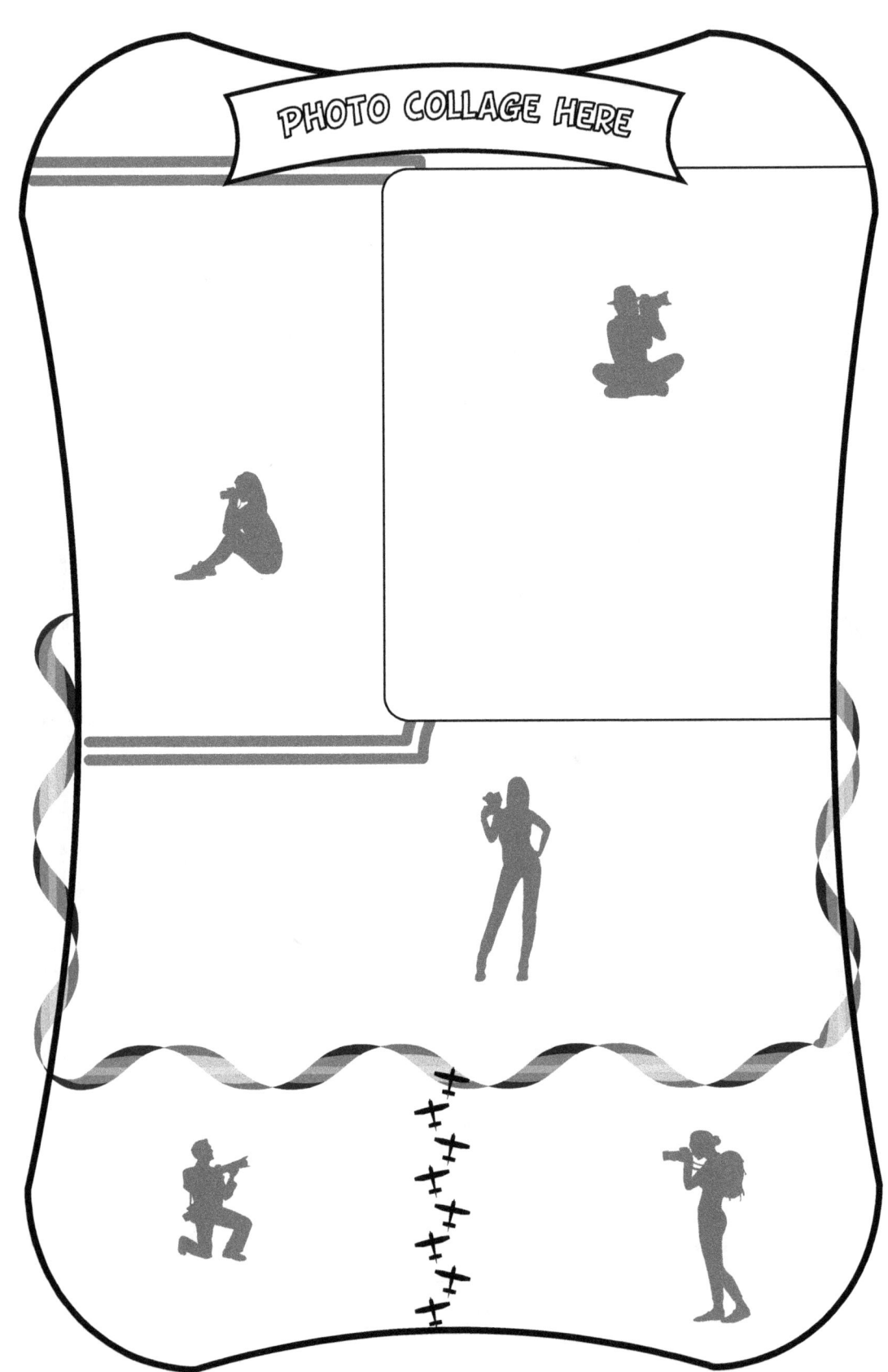

MY TRAVEL JOURNAL

Packing List

- ☐ Visa
- ☐ Passport
- ☐ Tickets
- ☐ ID's
- ☐ Credit Card
- ☐ Camera
- ☐ Chargers
- ☐ Sunglasses
- ☐ Shoes
- ☐ Slippers

Important Reminders

MY TRAVEL JOURNAL

Place to travel :

Hotel Reservation :

Travel Date :

Contact Person/Contact number :

Friends to see / visit :
-
-
-
-
-

Tour Guide :

Contact Person/Contact number :

Places to visti :
-
-
-
-
-
-

photo here

MY TRAVEL JOURNAL

Food Must Try

Shopping list

Food trip photo here

MY TRAVEL JOURNAL

the best part of this travel   **unforgettable memories**

journal

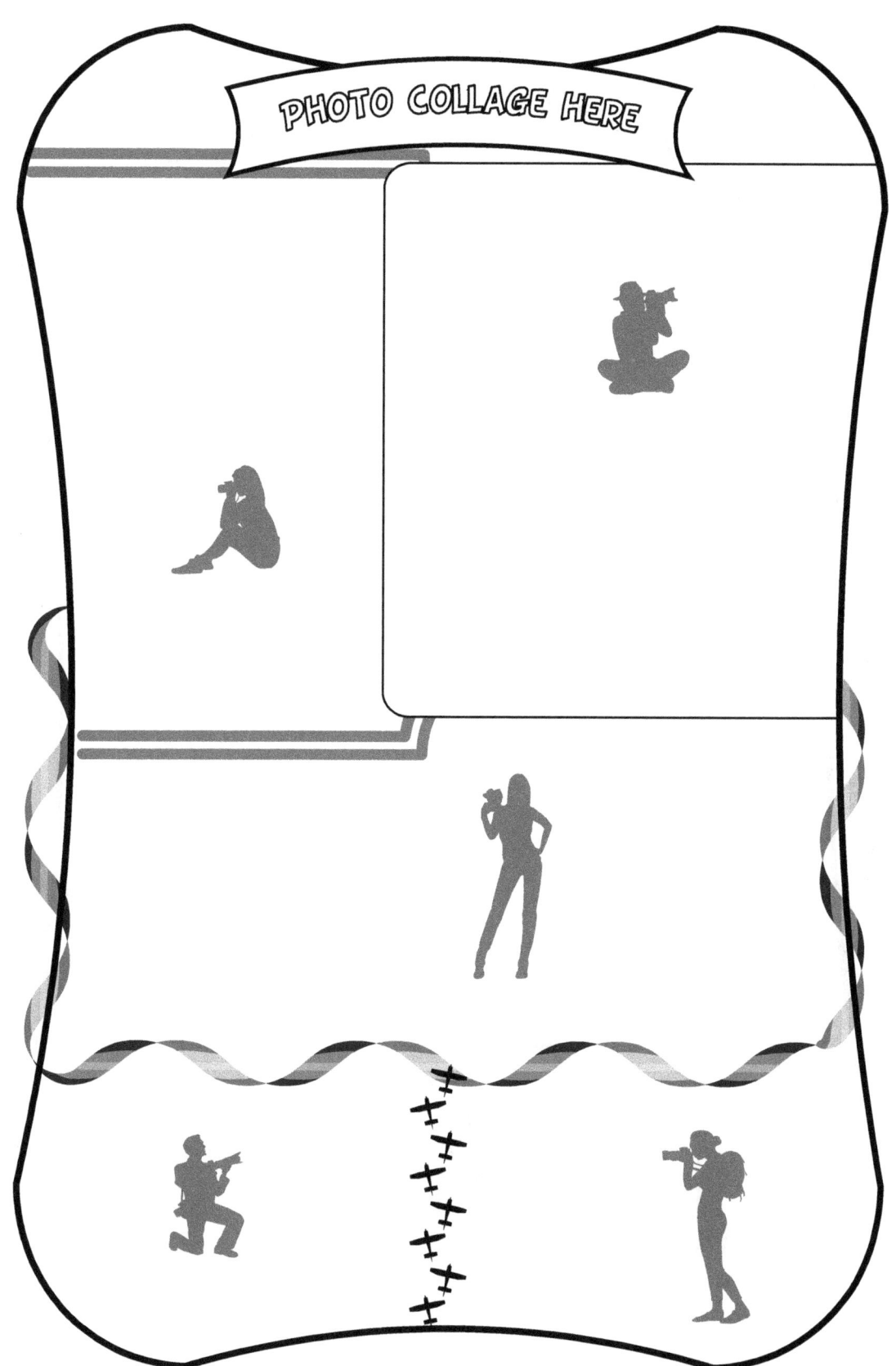

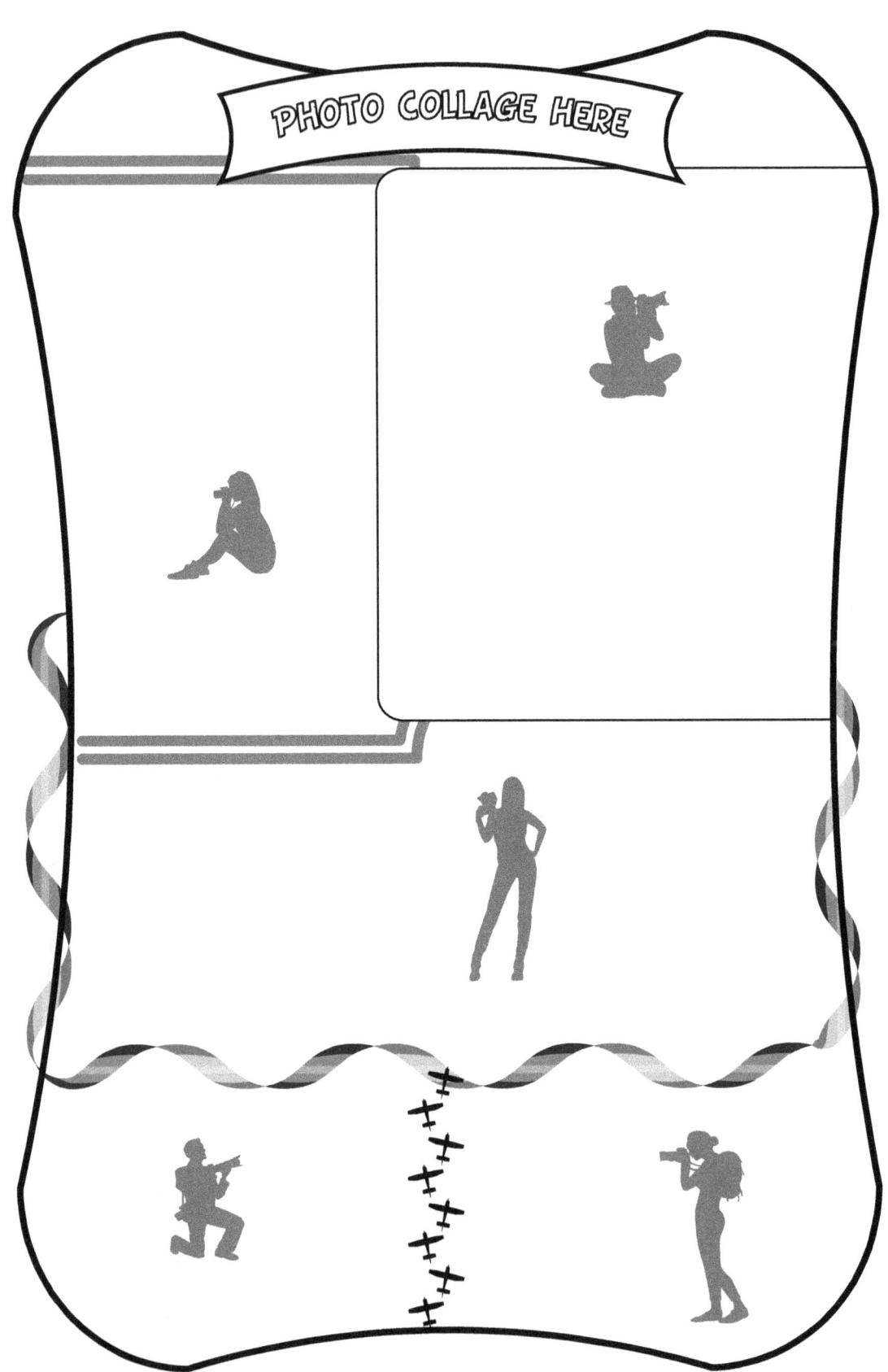

MY TRAVEL JOURNAL

Packing List

- ☐ Visa
- ☐ Passport
- ☐ Tickets
- ☐ ID's
- ☐ Credit Card
- ☐ Camera
- ☐ Chargers
- ☐ Sunglasses
- ☐ Shoes
- ☐ Slippers

Important Reminders

MY TRAVEL JOURNAL

Hotel Reservation :

Contact Person/Contact number :

Tour Guide :

Contact Person/Contact number :

Place to travel :

Travel Date :

Friends to see / visit :
-
-
-
-
-

Places to visti :
-
-
-
-
-
-

photo here

MY TRAVEL JOURNAL

Food Must Try

Shopping list

Food trip photo here

MY TRAVEL JOURNAL

the best part of this travel

unforgettable memories

journal

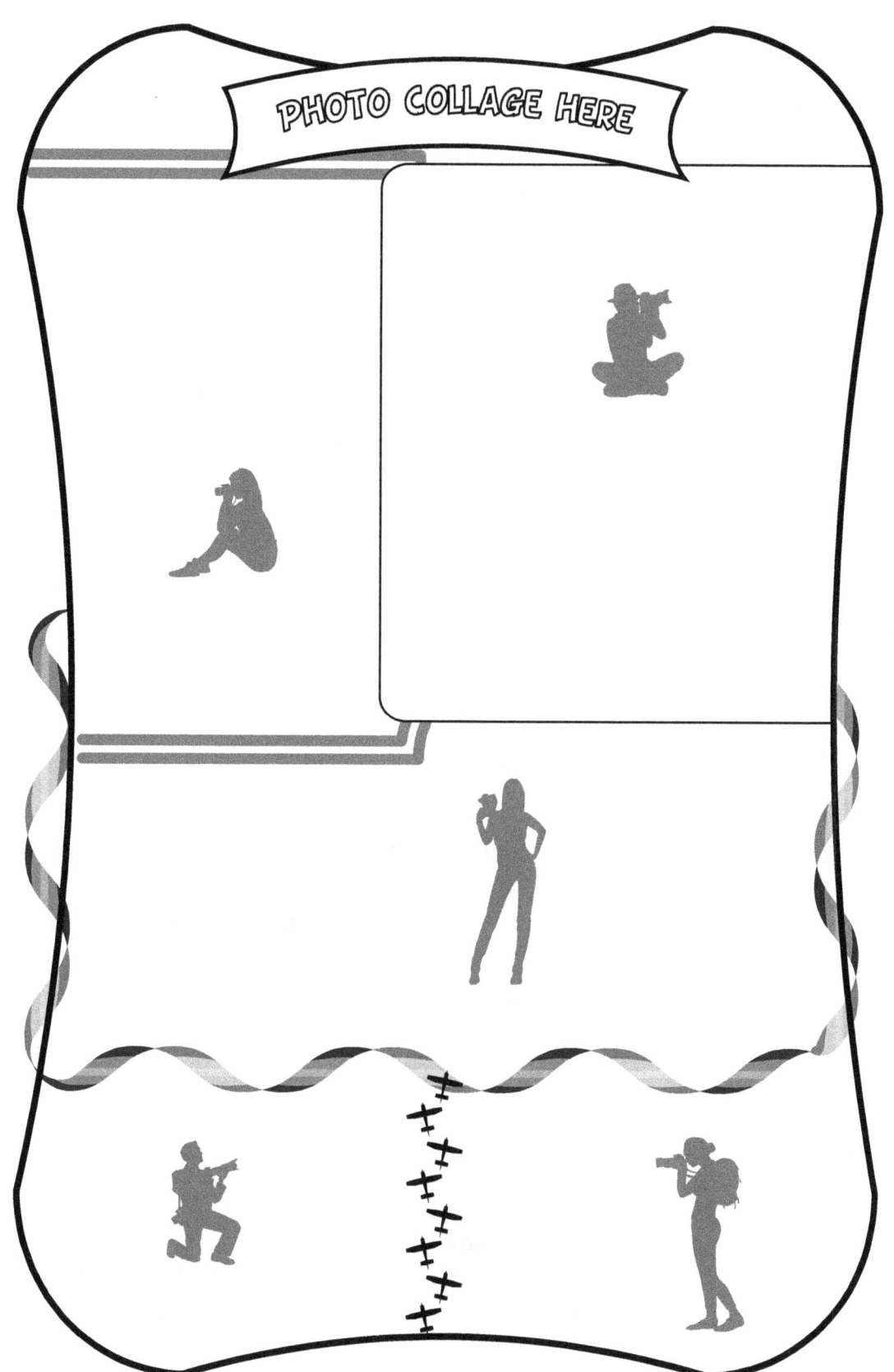

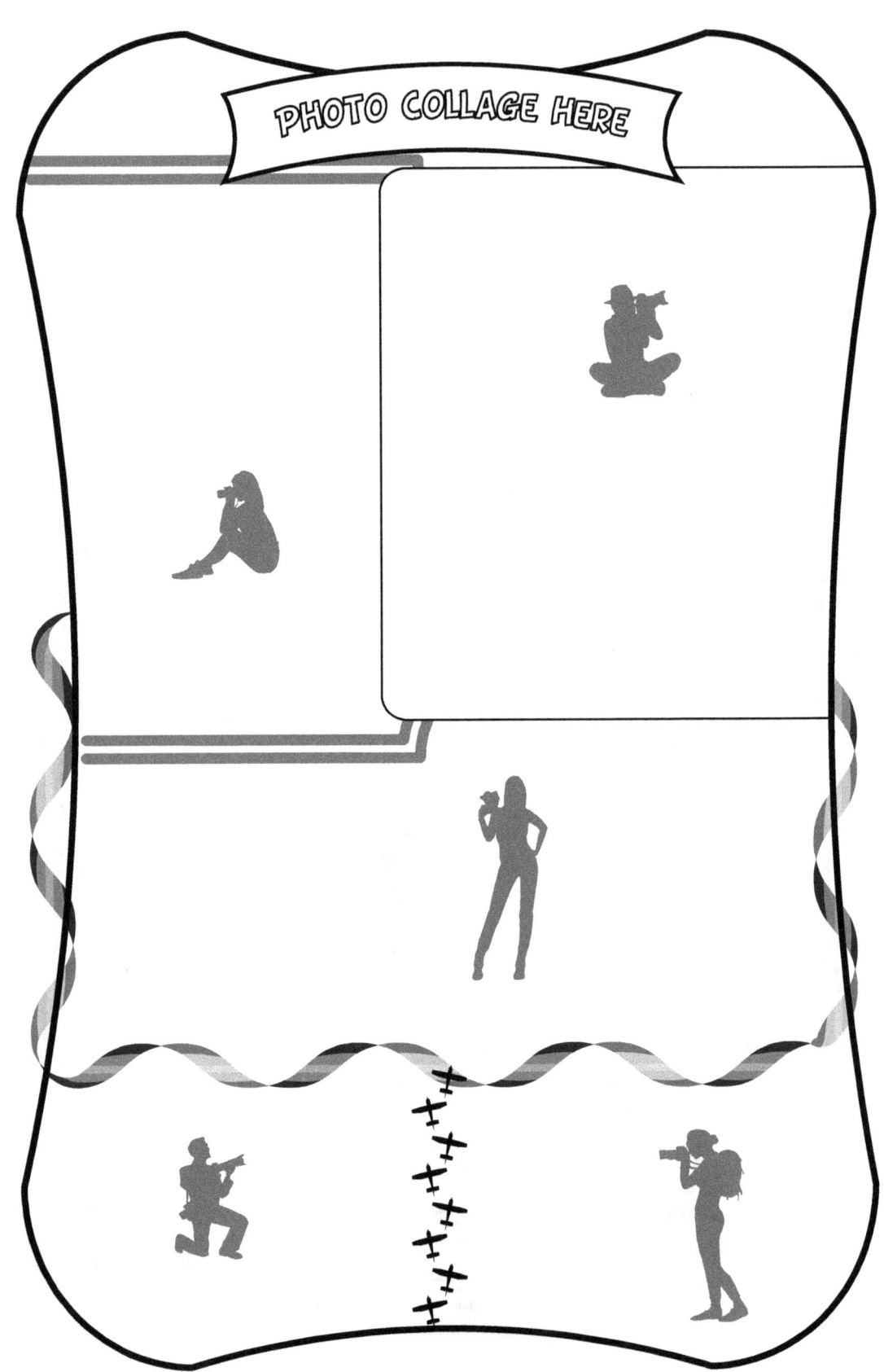

MY TRAVEL JOURNAL

Packing List

- ☐ Visa
- ☐ Passport
- ☐ Tickets
- ☐ ID's
- ☐ Credit Card
- ☐ Camera
- ☐ Chargers
- ☐ Sunglasses
- ☐ Shoes
- ☐ Slippers

Important Reminders

MY TRAVEL JOURNAL

Place to travel :

Hotel Reservation :

Travel Date :

Contact Person/Contact number :

Friends to see / visit :
-
-
-
-
-

Tour Guide :

Contact Person/Contact number :

Places to visti :
-
-
-
-
-
-

photo here

MY TRAVEL JOURNAL

Food Must Try

Shopping list

Food trip photo here

MY TRAVEL JOURNAL

the best part of this travel

unforgettable memories

journal

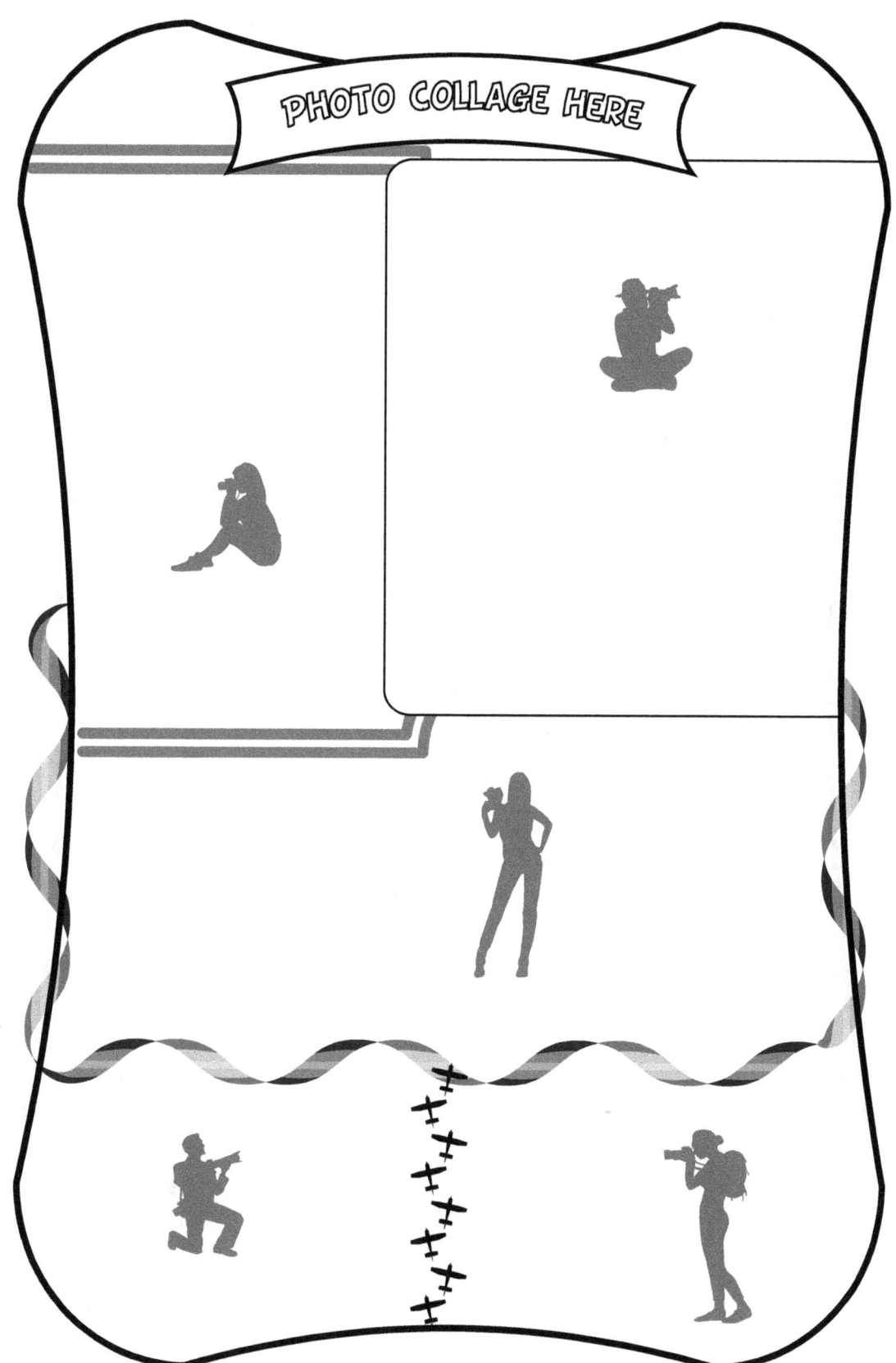

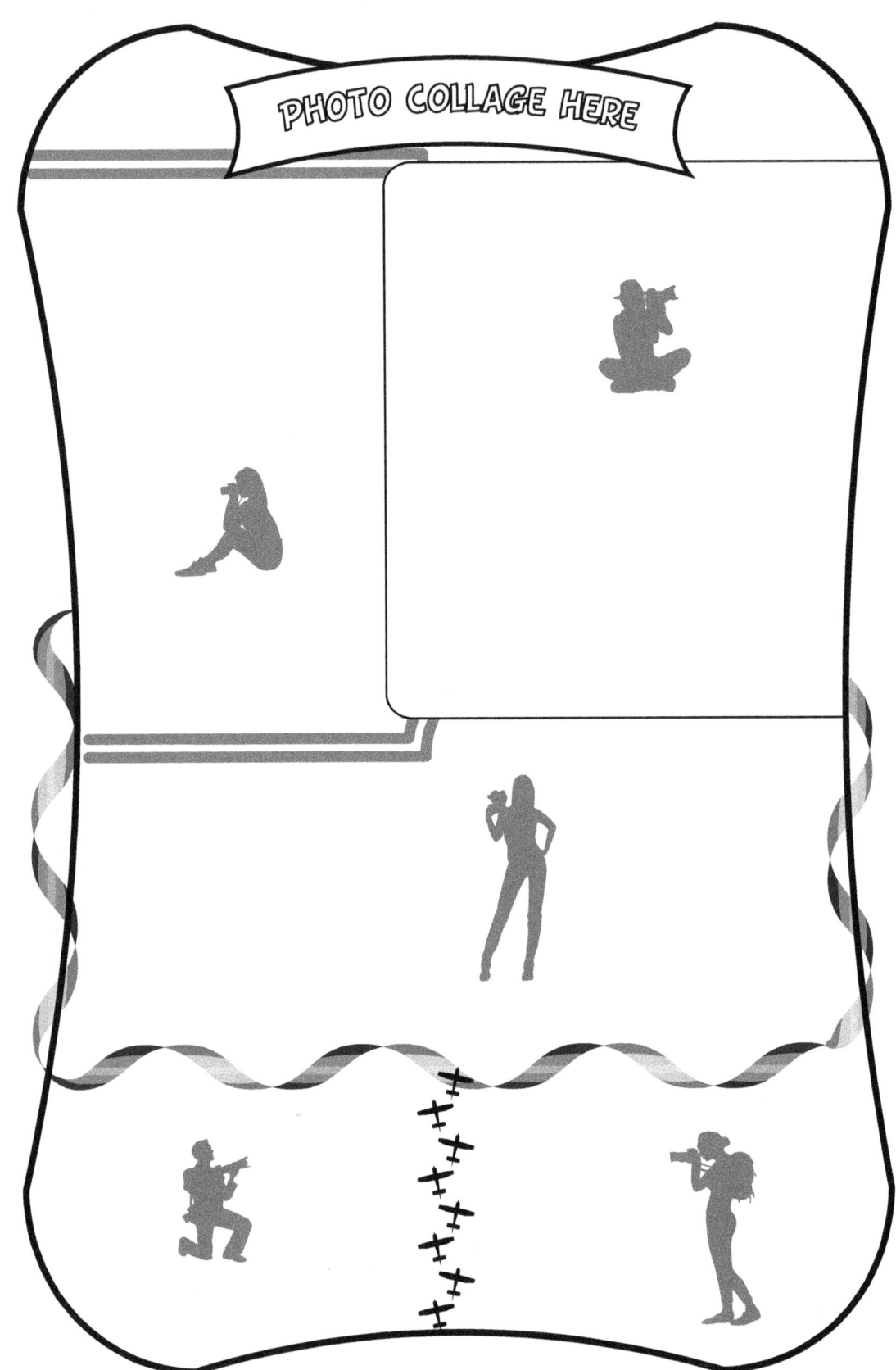

MY TRAVEL JOURNAL

Packing List

- ☐ Visa
- ☐ Passport
- ☐ Tickets
- ☐ ID's
- ☐ Credit Card
- ☐ Camera
- ☐ Chargers
- ☐ Sunglasses
- ☐ Shoes
- ☐ Slippers

Important Reminders

MY TRAVEL JOURNAL

Hotel Reservation :

Place to travel :

Travel Date :

Contact Person/Contact number :

Tour Guide :

Friends to see / visit :
-
-
-
-
-

Contact Person/Contact number :

Places to visti :
-
-
-
-
-
-

photo here

MY TRAVEL JOURNAL

Shopping list

Food Must Try

Food trip photo here

MY TRAVEL JOURNAL

the best part of this travel

unforgettable memories

journal

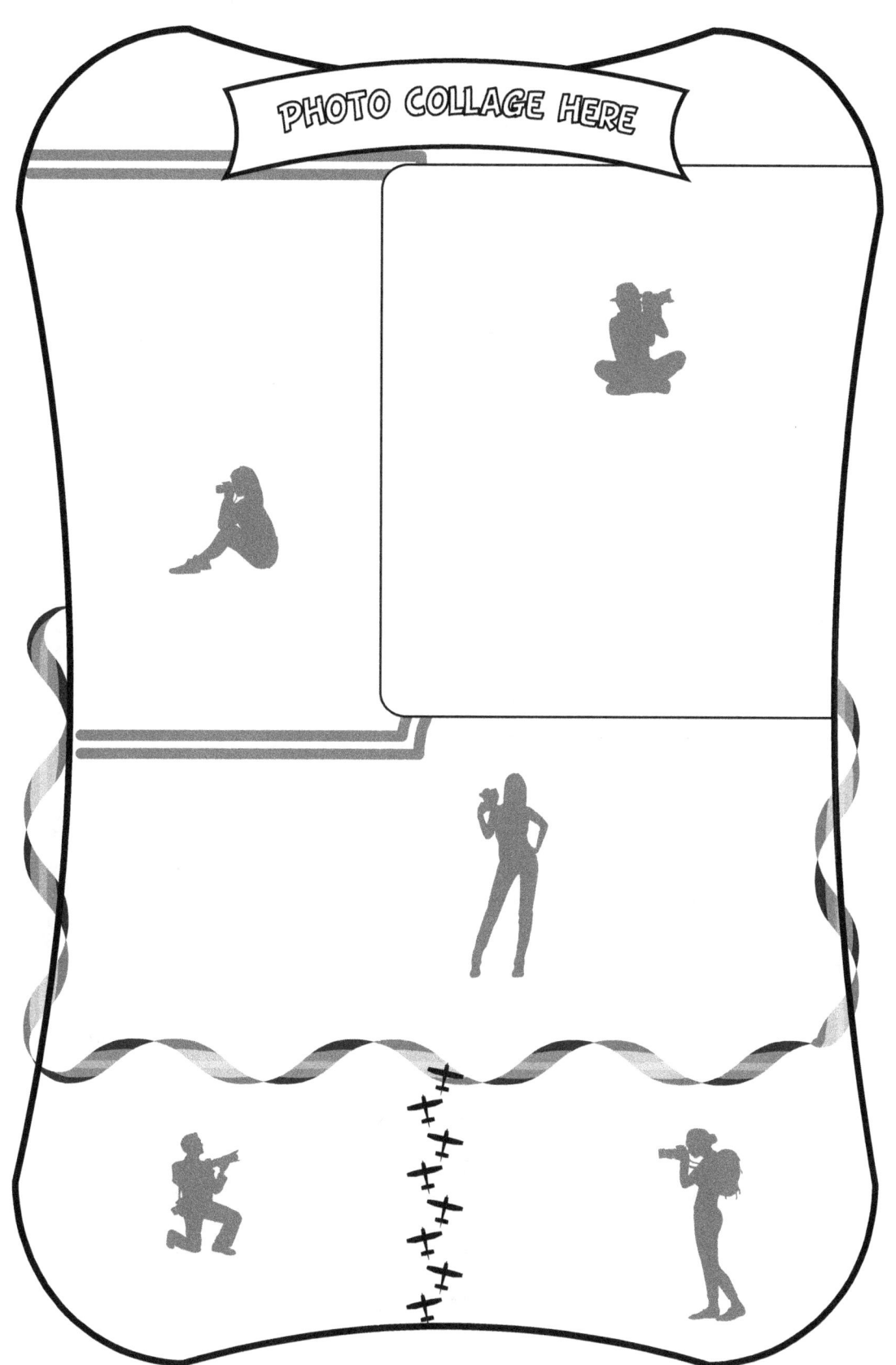
PHOTO COLLAGE HERE

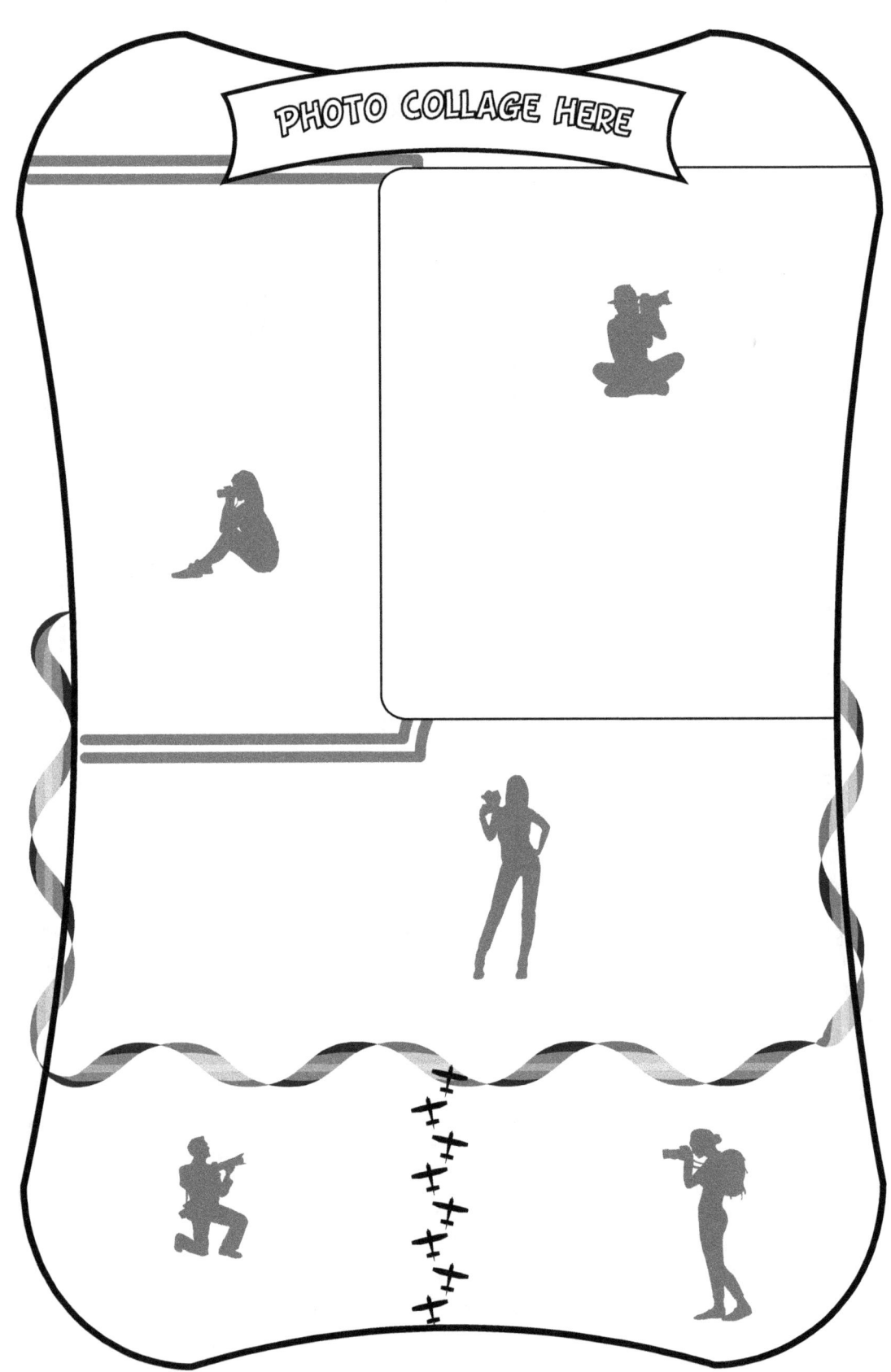

MY TRAVEL JOURNAL

Hotel Reservation :

Contact Person/Contact number :

Tour Guide :

Contact Person/Contact number :

Place to travel :

Travel Date :

Friends to see / visit :
-
-
-
-
-

Places to visti :
-
-
-
-
-

photo here

www.ingramcontent.com/pod-product-compliance
Lightning Source LLC
Chambersburg PA
CBHW081016040426
42444CB00014B/3230